GAME OF MY LIFE

LSU

TIGERS

GAME OF MY LIFE

LSU

TIGERS

MEMORABLE STORIES OF TIGERS FOOTBALL

MARTY MULÉ
FOREWORD BY PAUL DIETZEL

SPORTS
PUBLISHING

Sports Publishing books may be purchased in bulk at special discounts for sales promotion, corporate gifts, fund-raising, or educational purposes. Special editions can also be created to specifications. For details, contact the Special Sales Department, Sports Publishing, 307 West 36th Street, 11th Floor, New York, NY 10018 or info@skyhorsepublishing.com.

Sports Publishing® is a registered trademark of Skyhorse Publishing, Inc.®, a Delaware corporation.

www.sportspubbooks.com

10 9 8 7 6 5 4 3 2 1

Library of Congress Cataloging-in-Publication Data is available on file.

ISBN: 978-1-61321-008-6

Printed in the United States of America

For Richard Paul LaNasa, whose heart was always with the Tigers. And for Jo Jo, Katie, Carolina, and Conor, a litter of striped cubs.

CONTENTS

FOREWORD

Here we are, on the goal line with Max Fugler, Mike Anderson, and Ronnie Estay; flying downfield with Devery Henderson, Tommy Casanova and Billy Cannon; standing in the pocket with Bert Jones, Y.A. Tittle, and JaMarcus Russell. We're with Tommy Hodson the night the Tigers made the Earth shake, coming off the bench with Matt Mauck in an SEC title game, and following the blocking of Alan Faneca as we sprint with Herb Tyler to the end zone against No. 1-ranked Florida.

This living history of modern LSU football is one in which the reader goes on the field and into the huddle with the players—one in which the thoughts of central figures at the high points of their college careers and their reflections years later are as much a part of the individual stories as their memorable exploits.

I've known and coached some of these players, and it was thrilling to be back on the sidelines with them. I didn't know some of the others, but I feel I do now with a greater appreciation of their accomplishments, having lived through these games as seen by them years later—and through the writing of Marty Mulé.

Throughout my career, I've dealt with some of the finest sportswriters around—Pete Finney, Hap Glaudi, Dan Hardesty, and Bud Montet in Louisiana; and Til Ferdenzi, Allison Danzig, Tim Cohane and Red Smith in New York. Marty, a true disciple of Finney, is in their league. He has a wonderful and insightful knowledge of LSU athletics, with a writing style that conveys the feeling that "You were there" at many of the storied events of the past—not just a rote restatement of the facts but an exciting passion for the moment.

When he told me his project involved talking to the living players from LSU's most remembered games, my interest was piqued. When I read the finished work, I was delighted. Some of these games are classics that will forever live in LSU lore, as will many of these athletes.

To get the feelings of the actual players sets this book in a class by itself. You get to feel their exuberance, the thrill of victory, even the excruciating agony of a razor-thin defeat against an All-World team in which the Tigers rose mightily to the occasion.

There is no greater thrill than to be in the locker room with a team after a hard-fought game. Here, in this book, we are all there together: players, coaches, fans, and readers. It's a fun, satisfying, and meaningful experience.

Has anyone ever attended an LSU game without getting goosebumps as that Golden Band from Tigerland marches on the field playing its signature "Fan Fare"? The athletes on these pages raise goosebumps, too, just as does the spectacle and color of a Saturday night in Tiger Stadium—loud and very partisan.

The LSU passion for the Tigers goes far beyond the thrill of victory. As re-lived in these accounts of notable LSU games, the absolute frenzy generated in Tiger Stadium is without compare. This book gets to the "Heart of the Beast." This huge and constant display of emotion is the reason so many coaches feel Tiger Stadium is the most difficult site of all for opponents to play. That comes through, too, as part of this work.

But the heart of it is the faithful recounting of the exploits, the exuberance, and the disappointment of some of LSU's legends. Their inner feelings and their fights through difficulties are inspiring, remarkable moments in the lives of remarkable men.

Game of My Life LSU Tigers has really struck an inner chord with some of LSU's finest.

Paul Dietzel
Coach of the Fightin' Tigers, 1955-1961

ACKNOWLEDGMENTS

Ed Cassiere for his keen eye; Jim Kleinpeter, Ted Lewis, and Mike Triplett of *The New Orleans Times-Picayune*; Butch Muir of the *Baton Rouge Advocate*; Charles Bloom of the Southeastern Conference; Peter Finney of *The New Orleans Times-Picayune*; and Dan Hardesty of the *Baton Rouge State-Times*, whose on-the-scene reportage put some of these players in the games of their respective lives in clear focus.

The Chinese Bandits, colorful ancestors of modern LSU football.

INTRODUCTION

LSU is the heart of Louisiana. John J. McKeithen, the late governor and No. 1 Tiger fan, was convinced of that.

"Even when things go bad in the Pelican State," McKeithen said, in words recounted later on these pages, "something would happen at LSU that will lift the spirits of these sports-loving citizens." It's a statement backed by LSU's across-the-board 43 national championships, the most of all Southeastern Conference schools.

It's also a statement backed by the latest example, the gritty performance of the Tigers in the aftermath of Hurricane Katrina's devastation.

Each of these games is a drama in itself, and people like Billy Cannon, Jim Taylor, JaMarcus Russell, Dalton Hilliard, Bert Jones, Tommy Casanova, Charles Alexander, and Leonard Marshall are the definition of football heroes. Some, like Ken Kavanaugh, are heroes on the field and bigger heroes in life.

It was fun to hold Ole Miss, Auburn, and Notre Dame at the goal line again, exciting to feel the Earth under Tiger Stadium shaking again, and experience the ear-splitting noise as LSU beat—finally beat—a No. 1-ranked opponent.

There may never have been an interception for the Tigers so important as Marcus Spears' against Oklahoma in the Sugar Bowl to nail down the national championship—unless, of course, it was Jerry Joseph's in the Cotton Bowl against Arkansas in perhaps the greatest LSU victory of all.

To relive these moments with the men who made them happen was a thrill. This wasn't my idea, but it was one that hooked me as soon as it was prosposed. This was not only an intriguing but an intoxicating project for someone who grew up hearing about the legends of LSU football, later watching and reading about those who followed, then spending a third of a century observing and reporting on yet other Tigers leaving their own indelible marks on the sports memory bank of Louisiana. The idea of taking a personal journey through what became essentially a history of modern LSU football—eight decades from the pre-World War II era with Kavanaugh's spectacular game against Holy Cross to Russell's exploits at Arizona State with the horrors of Katrina as a backdrop—was more than appealing. To produce *Game of My Life: LSU* required probing the thoughts of major figures before, during, and after that event that is so embedded in their minds. It also called for putting the circumstances of the individual—and his team—at the time, the game was played in focus. Then, as important as anything, finding where they each went from that highpoint to the rest of their respective lives.

Jerry Stovall went from being an All-American at LSU to an All-Pro career with the St. Louis Cardinals, then coaching at his alma mater. He's now CEO of a Baton Rouge sports foundation. But as much as anything, finding that his main concern upon reaching the end zone on his memorable kickoff return against Georgia Tech was his ill father-in-law was, to say the least, surprising. So was learning that Mike Anderson called the wrong defensive alignment on the goal line against Auburn, leading to the do-or-die tackle that earned him permanent reverence at LSU. Or that JaMarcus Russell spotted something during his last-gasp heroics at Arizona State that his coaches didn't see until studying the film days later, something that allowed the Tigers to escape Arizona State with an improbable win—a victory in which Russell never had any doubt.

Thank you, Tigers, for sharing with me a glimpse of your personal athletic highlights from the Games of your Lives—and so much more.

MJM
March 15, 2006

CHAPTER 1

CHARLES ALEXANDER

LSU 56 - Oregon 17
October 22, 1977 • Tiger Stadium

Charlie Alexander was bruised, tired, and a little bewildered when he heard his name called.

Late in a game where he'd already left his mark, Alexander was ordered back on the field where the gathering of reserves who had been playing since midway through the third quarter awaited.

On the game's last play, Alexander bolted two yards into the end zone for a touchdown.

His name was now etched in the LSU record book. No Tiger had ever before run for four touchdowns. In fact, no Tiger had ever before had as many carries, 31, or run for as many yards, 237, as Alexander did that night. More than a quarter-century would pass before another Tiger would.

"I didn't know why I was sent back," Alexander said. "But I was happy to know I had done something that had never been done here before."

But Rich Brooks wasn't happy. "I wish that he'd broken his leg," the Ducks' coach said sourly, believing LSU had run up the score on him.

Paul Manasseh, the Tigers' sports information director, was to blame. McClendon sat Alexander down after he passed Terry Robiskie's

No. 4 was "Alexander the Great" to the Tigers.

one-year-old rushing record of 214 yards. Manasseh realized the junior had an opportunity to set the school record for touchdowns rushing, and called down to the field to inform McClendon, who immediately sent his tailback into the game.

"I did it because I have an obligation to my team," McClendon said later. "I have an obligation to my team and to Charles. I apologized to Coach Brooks and our fans after we did it, but you just don't know when a chance like that will come along again."

Not often—that school record has been equaled and surpassed just one time since.

The oddity is that LSU, 4-2 afterward, did not play an exceptional game against Brooks' 1-5 Ducks. LSU lost five fumbles, none initiated by contact. Oregon took a 7-0 lead before the Tigers got untracked and took a 21-7 lead by the half, then blew it open in the second half, when Alexander scored all his touchdowns on jaunts of 2, 20, 4, and 2 yards. All told, LSU amassed a school-record 503 yards rushing, which would be an attention-drawing effort against anybody, even against tall weeds.

Alexander, who had averaged 7.6 yards against the Ducks, was Brooks' biggest problem, the Oregon coach said later.

"We couldn't stop him," Brooks admitted. "We tried, but he's just a tremendous back. There might not be a better one around."

* * *

St. Mark wrote: "One came running."

That was the gospel at LSU in the mid-1970s, the memorable years of Alexander in the Tiger backfield.

He wasn't from Macedonia—he came out of Galveston, Texas—but at LSU, he was Alexander the Great, a runner who left nine SEC records and 27 LSU records in his wake.

Alexander ranks with the very best who ever carried a ball at LSU—Doc Fenton, Steve Van Buren, Jimmy Taylor, Billy Cannon, Jerry Stovall, Dalton Hilliard, Kevin Faulk.

"He looks good in a hotel lobby," former Dallas Cowboys personnel director Gil Brandt sighed.

Yet, no one had to come from so far behind to make a dent on the charts. To say the 6-foot, 1-inch, 215-pound Alexander had an inauspicious start would be understating the obvious. In his first two varsity games, as the backup to Terry Robiskie, Alexander had a net gain of one yard in 16 carries against Nebraska and Texas A&M.

By comparison, Alexander's teammate Robiskie, at the same point in his Tiger career, had 77 rushing yards. Billy Cannon had 211, Art Cantrelle 103, Brad Davis 53. By the end of the '75 season, however, Alexander had made inroads, slight though they may have seemed at the time. An 81-yard game against Tulane in the finale gave Alexander 301 yards on 108 carries as a freshman.

"Against Nebraska [a 10-7 loss] he carried the ball a total of eight times for a minus-two yards. McClendon recalled. "In the dressing room, I patted him on the back and said, 'Charlie, things are going to get better.' He just looked at me and didn't say a word. Then came that real fine bunch from Texas A&M [a 39-8 defeat], and he carried eight times for plus-three [yards]. So here's a total of 16 carries for one yard. I kept patting him on the back and saying, 'Things are going to get better.' Now we can laugh, look back, and say that things really did get better."

That they did.

Alexander's first 100-yard-plus performance came against Vanderbilt (152) in the fifth game of his sophomore year. A 138-yard game against Ole Miss and 141 against Utah filled out the muscular Texan's seasonal stats to 876 yards on 155 carries as the Tigers began to depend more and more on their hammerin' reserve tailback.

Flashes of immense potential began to show as Alexander spelled Robiskie. "If he ever learns to run under control," observers said, "Alexander could develop into more than just a good back." He blossomed just when LSU needed it most, spearheading the Tigers to their first bowl in three years, the Sun Bowl in El Paso.

To compound matters, the 1977 Tiger defense bore little resemblance to the brick walls upon which McClendon's reputation was built. Possession, buying time for the defense, became as much the responsibility of the offense as scoring.

"The Root Hogs," the offensive line composed of men who were far more students than athletes (including tackle Robert Dugas, now an

Statisticians had a hard time keeping up with Charles Alexander.

M.D.; tackle Chris Rich, also an M.D.; center Jay Whitley, a dentist; and novelist John Ed Bradley, who backed up Whitley), vowed to burrow as many traffic lanes for Alexander as possible. Alexander was clearly the linchpin of this team, and the Root Hogs were going to give him every opportunity to lead them to victory. A joke began around Broussard Hall—then the athletic dormitory—that Alexander wouldn't go into his room unless the door was opened by one of the Root Hogs.

The battering ram onslaught left tattered and bruised defenses in its aftermath. Statisticians, however, may have had the most difficult task of 1977—keeping up with Charlie Alexander.

He set school records for most rushing yards in a single game (237); touchdowns in a single game (4); carries in a single game (43); carries for a season (311); touchdowns in a season (17); yards rushing in a season (1,686); most yards averaged in a season (153.3).

The 1,686 yards came principally from tackle to tackle, in the pit, and was accomplished with only one run as long as 43 yards.

"That's the incredible thing about him," said Vic Eumont, then a Tulane assistant. "I've seen backs I felt were better breakaway threats. But not many who can take the pounding Charlie Alexander takes 20, 30, 40 times a game and still come back ready to do it again.

"I don't think I was really all that impressed with him [in 1976] until we started seeing film on him. He runs high, so he really takes some shots. But he doesn't fumble, and he doesn't get hurt."

The man who appreciated Alexander the most was, of course, the one who kept telling him things would get better, McClendon.

"Make sure to capitalize the 'G' on great," Charlie Mac said, "because that's exactly what he was for us."

* * *

Alexander went on to a pro career, where he played in Super Bowl XVI for the Cincinnati Bengals.

Now he works in Houston as a sales representative for oil field equipment—"Very hard," he said—to get two daughters through college, one at Harvard Law School.

He doesn't remember many details of the Oregon game, except that it was his entrée to the record books.

"It was big at the time," Alexander said, "but it really wasn't *that* big, if you know what I mean. Now, when I look back on it, with maturity and the perspective of years, I think, 'Man, did I really do all that?'"

He sure did.

CHAPTER 2

MIKE
ANDERSON

LSU 17 - Auburn 9
October 24, 1970 • Auburn, Alabama

Mike Anderson stood anchored ankle-deep in the mud, half in and half out of the end zone and seemingly all alone as a blue-shirted locomotive steamed right at him.

"Oh, God," he remembers thinking, "I'd better not screw this up."

In a do-or-die situation with four minutes remaining, Anderson, thankfully, didn't. The LSU linebacker hit Auburn runner Wallace Clark shoulder-high and square in the chest, stopping him a foot away from the end zone—and a possible two-point conversion away from an unsatisfying tie instead of a very satisfying upset of a two-touchdown favorite.

Not natural or frequent rivals at the time, this was LSU's first game at Auburn in 62 seasons. Not since the great Tiger team of 1908, an undefeated point-a-minute juggernaut which beat Auburn 10-2, had LSU played on the Alabama plains—and this was going to be no easy task.

Auburn was unbeaten after five games, ranked No. 6, and averaging 35 points a game. Every time he handled the ball, run or pass, quarterback Pat Sullivan was averaging nine yards. Things wouldn't be any better for LSU on the other side of the ball either.

Auburn had a formidable defense, the SEC's third best overall—tops against the pass.

What LSU had going for it was the SEC's best defense, knowledge the Tigers could hang with Auburn (they won 21-20 in a classic the year before in Baton Rouge)—and torrential rains.

"It was so bad," Anderson recalled, "we literally were standing ankle-deep in water. We couldn't see the other side of the field. They had the Sullivan-to-[Terry] Beasley passing combination, but we had the nation's best run defense. The weather sure wasn't going to hurt us."

All that was separating LSU from the kind of season it had in '69, when the Tigers were awesome defensively, was a flukey loss in the opener against Texas A&M when a sophomore cornerback made a sophomore mistake in the fading minutes and went for an interception instead of the tackle. The receiver went for 79 yards and a touchdown with seconds to play to give the Aggies a 20-18 victory. Since then, however, LSU won four in a row, a stretch in which Anderson was twice named the SEC's lineman of the week.

In a memorable 1968 performance against Kentucky, in which Anderson, then a sophomore, made 15 tackles, five inside the Tiger 5 to help secure a 13-3 LSU victory, an observer told Tiger coach Charlie McClendon, "You know you have the best linebacker in the country."

Charlie Mac answered simply, "I know."

* * *

Standing tall on the goal line was nothing new for Anderson. That's where he was in 1968 when defending Southwest Conference champion Texas A&M—with the nation's longest winning streak at eight—opened the season at LSU. The 13-12 game came down to the last minutes with a tackle just short of the goal line by teammates Carlos Rabb and Gerry Kent, stripping the back from the ball, which rolled out of the end zone for a touchback and allowed LSU to run out the clock. He was also shoulder to shoulder with George Bevan in 1969 when Bevan blocked a late PAT attempt by Auburn to save a 21-20 LSU victory.

"Oh, yeah," Anderson said. "I'd been in a lot of those kinds of situations before."

Mike Anderson was the anchor of the LSU defense.

And seen them, too. As a 10-year-old, Mike was at the 1959 LSU-Ole Miss game when Billy Cannon blazed 89 yards across the field with his famed punt return, then helped save the day with a tackle at the LSU-1 with 18 seconds to go.

"I was kind of an LSU nut," Anderson said. "My dad had season tickets, and I remember sitting with him on the east side end upper-deck and being able to watch Cannon run all the way down those sidelines."

The stopping of Ole Miss took place on the other side of the stadium, but the emotion of that last tackle sent shivers up and down the spine of the youngster, who had already made up his mind there would nothing finer in life than to grow up and play for the Tigers.

After a sterling prep career at Baton Rouge's Lee High, Anderson's services were in high demand. However, he said, "I didn't even make any [recruiting] trips."

Mike had been friends with Steve Dietzel, son of the former LSU coach, so when the senior Dietzel, then head coach at South Carolina, called to see if there was any interest, Anderson was not surprised—or even tempted. More startling was answering the phone and hearing the deep and charming growl of Alabama's Bear Bryant.

Anderson still wasn't interested.

He knew where he belonged—on the Tiger defense, guarding the end zone.

* * *

This was one of the most bizarre games LSU ever played. On the first play, Auburn mishandled the slippery ball, and LSU tackle Ronnie Estay recovered. It didn't take long for quarterback Buddy Lee to send a soaked spiral to Andy Hamilton in the end zone.

LSU was in front to stay, but the fun was just beginning.

In the second quarter, backup quarterback Bert Jones guided the Tigers 85 yards for another touchdown, this one by halfback Art Cantrelle. Every point in a game like this is important, and the Tigers ended up getting two on the PAT on a fortuitous play that the Keystone Kops could have executed. The snapped wet ball slipped past holder Paul Lyons, so kicker Mark Lumpkin picked it up, ran to one side, then—as he was about to be tackled—heaved it left-handed (though he is right-handed) towards the end zone. The ball was batted around before Lyons finally pulled it in and lunged over for the two points.

The Tigers got another two points in the final period when Estay, Buddy Millican, and John Sage cornered Sullivan in the Plainsmen's end zone.

The four points LSU garnered on those two plays meant in the final minutes Auburn, held to three field goals, was trying to salvage a tie, not going for the victory that could catapult it higher in the rankings.

Auburn wasn't going down easily. After a late drive, Sullivan had the Plainsmen at the LSU 8 with a first down.

"The funny thing," Anderson said, "is all of a sudden the sun came out. It was shining just as bright as could be as we made that stand."

On two of the next three plays, Anderson made the tackle. Auburn, however, was at the LSU 3 for its last shot. In what looked like a cat-and-mouse game between the offense and defense, a huge hole appeared on the right side of the defensive line. Sullivan called an audible and sent Clark barreling through.

"I called the wrong defense," Anderson, still horrified at the memory, said with a shake of the head. "I thought their offensive line had spread too much, so I stacked [tackle] John Sage in the gap, and I got behind him. When the play was called, John just happened to take the guard and tackle with him, and their end blocked out ours [Art Davis] and just left a giant hole.

"I knew I'd screwed up, and it was all up to me."

Clark went straight through the gap, where Anderson met him at the 1, stopping him cold.

"I really lucked up to stop him," Anderson said. "If he had been a little more shifty, maybe he would have gotten past me—but he wanted to run me over. I didn't let him."

"Nothing less than a perfect tackle by Anderson would have kept Auburn from scoring," McClendon said. "Auburn had blocked perfectly. Mike cheated over to middle linebacker. The hole was there, but Anderson met him head on. He stopped Clark as cold as you'll ever see a man stopped.

On goal-line stands, linebacker Mike Anderson stood tall.

"Our boys went over there to win," McClendon added. "They were determined, but nobody was ever more determined than Anderson when he hit Clark on that fourth-down play. I don't think I'll ever forget that."

* * *

In a season of big plays, Anderson's stands out. He finished the afternoon with six solo tackles, assisted on six more, and batted down a pass—factors that helped him at season's end when Anderson was a consensus All-American.

LSU went on to win the 1970 SEC championship and played in the Orange Bowl, losing 17-12 to Nebraska after the Cornhuskers turned a fourth-quarter fumble recovery into the winning touchdown.

That turned out to be Anderson's last game. Expected for a while to be a No. 1 draft choice, his three knee surgeries at LSU jeopardized any hope of a pro career. Appearing on the Bob Hope All-American Show, the comedian introduced Anderson by saying, "Mike has had so many knee operations he had one at halftime."

Anderson wasn't drafted until the ninth round, by Pittsburgh. After he was cut there, he tried out at several camps, but his knees wouldn't carry him.

"I couldn't cut anymore," he said. "My life's ambition was to play pro football," he said ruefully, "but I can't complain. My knees really were shot."

* * *

His name is still recognized throughout south Louisiana and Mississippi.

"The difference is," Anderson said, "is that older fans remember me as a football player. Younger people hear my name and think of a restaurant."

Anderson operates five seafood eateries, which rank among the most popular in the area. The change of life from football to restaurateur took a while.

"I tried a little of everything," Anderson said. "I tried farming, health clubs, specialty advertising."

In 1975 Anderson was selling concrete. While traveling one day on Baton Rouge's Highland Road, near the south gates of LSU, he spotted an old grocery store. Anderson had been mulling over the possibility of opening a seafood market. He stopped in the store, the owner was in, and he asked if he might consider renting to Anderson. He would.

"So I opened," Anderson said with a laugh. "I had no idea what I was doing. I was selling raw seafood, boiling some, and making about four kinds of po-boys. At first we didn't even have a knife to cut the bread, that's how much I knew. I even had my poor dad in there, trying to boil crabs, with no ventilation in the room."

Anderson's dad and his banker, who was a close friend, both tried to talk Mike into giving up the business. "I told them I'm kind of out of options. Just hang with me a little longer and maybe we can do something."

It took a little longer. One day before an LSU game, he made about 200 po-boys and tried to get the word out, figuring maybe people would pick them up before kickoff.

"We did zero business,"Anderson said. After the game that night he sat near the road as traffic left Tiger Stadium and, to any car with the windows down, he threw the wrapped po-boys in.

Eventually people from Collegetown, an area of apartments and convenience stores, started coming in. Business started to grow ... and grow ... and grow. ...

"We started expanding, both the menus and the restaurant," Anderson said. In explaining what a shoestring operation it first was, he said he liked to experiment with the food. One of his best-selling dishes today is a crabmeat étouffée.

Mike was in the kitchen one day, working with a combination of crabmeat and speckled trout, and overcooked the dish.

"Me and the staff all tried it, and everybody liked it a lot," Anderson said. They decided to add it to their menu, but no one could think of a name for the dish. At that moment, Norman, the air-conditioning repairman came walking through the kitchen.

Today one of the most popular dishes at Mike Anderson's Seafood Restaurants is "The Norman."

CHAPTER 3

JOHN ED BRADLEY

Southern Cal 17 - LSU 12
September 29, 1979 • Tiger Stadium

John Ed Bradley left everything he had on the field against Southern Cal—or at least a lot of what he had to give.

"Before the game," he recalled, "I weighed in at 243 pounds. Afterward I stepped on the scale, and I was 221. That's 22 pounds, all of them melted into the grass of Tiger Stadium."

Along with the hearts of every other Tiger—that's how monumental, how rousing, their effort really was.

This was that heartbreaking night when, for 59 minutes and 28 seconds of searing emotional football, LSU held the team of its worst nightmares at bay.

That game was such an inspiration that, in LSU lore, it now holds the same kind of mythic quality as the Alamo does for Texans.

This is how much it meant: 22 years after it was played, and on his deathbed, in a raspy voice, Charlie McClendon asked Bradley if he ever thought back to the '79 USC game.

"I remember it all the time," Bradley, captain of that Tiger team, said. "I don't always want to remember it, because we lost, Coach, but I remember it."

Bradley wrote of that last visit with Charlie Mac in a *Sports Illustrated* story entitled: "The Best Years of His Life".

Three days before Charlie Mac took leave of this world, even before he asked the question, he was remembering, too. That's how valiant was the effort of his Tigers.

* * *

There may never have been a game when any LSU team played as much to its potential—maybe even beyond—than that evening the when the out-manned Tigers held USC to a near-standstill.

No. 1-ranked Southern California was perhaps the best team in terms of sheer talent ever to set cleats in Tiger Stadium. Two Heisman Trophy winners (Charles White in '79 and Marcus Allen in '81), the Lombardi Award winner in Brad Budde, future Hall of Famers Ronnie Lott in the secondary and Anthony Munoz on the line, 12 All-Americans, 12 first-round draft choices and 31 athletes who would spend at least one season in the NFL suited up that day for the Trojans.

That, folks, was one serious football team. And what was LSU going to throw at the mighty Trojans? A not particularly big, not especially fast SEC team—one just decent by SEC standards—but a motivated one. This was the last band of Tigers under McClendon, undone by the school's interfering Board of Supervisors, which seemed to think LSU should be unbeaten—every season. In any case, his team wanted to give Charlie Mac a season, a game, something to remember for his 18 mostly sterling years.

It wasn't likely to be against Southern Cal, which already was being called College Football's Team of the Half Century in some quarters.

"They were what we call now 'The Next Generation' of athlete," Bradley said. "Except this was then. USC was the first team with that kind of athletes across the board, big but with speed—fast but with size."

Center John Ed Bradley was captain of the '79 Tigers.

The Trojans were indeed big, with the average starting offensive lineman coming in at 6 feet, 5 inches, 255 pounds, which meant USC's line was NFL size and would have averaged 12 pounds more than the defensive line of the '79 New Orleans Saints. That, of course, is not to mention 27 pounds a man more than LSU's defensive line and linebackers.

To put that USC team in individual terms: on some plays LSU's Benji Thibodeaux, at 6 feet, 2 inches, 242 pounds, would have to take on both Budde and Van Horn—all 505 pounds of them.

"It's not just that they weigh so much," assessed Charlie McClendon at the time. "It's also that they're so tall. They're like a basketball team. When they run that sweep, finding White will be like finding a sports car behind a lot of buses."

The Trojans were 3-0 and a 12-point favorite against the 2-0 Tigers, who didn't know how good or how average they were, having beaten Colorado and Rice, two average teams at best. But things didn't look good, according to one NFL observer who noted LSU had no legitimate superstars to compare with the gifted behemoths of Troy. "LSU has only two players who, as they say, can make things happen: wide receiver Carlos Carson and cornerback Chris Williams," was his assessment.

McClendon had another serious concern, though he kept his comments confined to his team. "I told my team all week even a five-yard penalty could be the difference—and I told them we were playing the holdingest team in football."

* * *

Raucous fans vented steam, rocking Tiger Stadium long before the kickoff. They'd been waiting for a shot at ambushing USC ever since the game was announced several years before.

When the Trojans came on the field, the sound of the disapproving partisans was jarring. When the first glint of the flood lights on the gold helmets standing in the home team chute was spotted, the screams and yells started building. When the beloved Tigers finally rushed on the field, the decibels were at shattering levels. From then to game's end, the quietest moment in the stadium was a low roar.

"The noise level is always a factor at Tiger Stadium," Bradley, the center, said, "but that night it exceeded anything I'd ever heard. The sound was like a physical force. Everything was just a howl. Of course, it was problem for USC, but it was for us, too. We didn't call signals in that game. Everyone just watched me and plays were simply run on my snap."

Bradley had other responsibilities as well. Not only did he have to handle nose guard Ty Sperling, but USC used the gifted Lott in many ways, almost as a linebacker at times, and often on blitzes. In those instances, he would become Bradley's responsibility.

"I knew I would have to play better than I ever did just to hold my own," Bradley said.

He did, and every man on the LSU team did.

* * *

Despite the fact that the Trojans jumped in front early with a field goal, the Tigers almost immediately stirred the adrenalin of the crowd. They not only showed no signs of playing the sacrificial lamb, but actually inched in front.

"Once we took their first punch," Bradley said, "we were okay. We felt we could play with them."

On a 3rd-and-13, quarterback Steve Ensminger speared a galloping Tracy Porter for 15 yards, down to the USC 36. Jude Hernandez then busted through the middle for 24 yards on a perfect trap call, as Lott, playing rover, charged into the backfield on a blitz.

Two calls later, Ensminger hit a wide-open LeRoid Jones (in the lineup because LSU's first two tailbacks, Hokie Gajan and Hernandez, were injured early), who was playing slot-left, in the middle of the end zone. The conversion was botched.

But, after Charles White fumbled a few minutes later, LSU increased its lead to 9-3 on a 32-yard field goal by Don Barthels.

That the Tigers were not only in the hunt but actually in the lead as the halftime whistle blew was a testament to their disciplined enthusiasm—and the denizens of Tiger Stadium were whipped into an emotional frenzy.

And the Tigers kept coming. Second-team quarterback David Woodley drove LSU to the USC-2, but eventually had to settle for another Barthels field goal.

The place was in bedlam.

Someone should have sensed what was coming, though, because the Tigers were leaving too many precious points on the goal line, getting three-point field goals instead of six-point touchdowns.

On top of that, a golden opportunity slipped through LSU's fingers when Paul McDonald, under a heavy rush on third-and-five from the USC 30, threw a pass in the flat. Cornerback Chris Williams was there, waiting, with clear sailing to the end zone.

"I had it all the way," Williams said later. "Coach Mac always tells us to never take our eye off the ball. This time I did. The ball went right through my hands. If I catch it, I could have walked in."

Shortly afterward, the revitalized Trojans got the ball at their 43 and drove to a touchdown in six plays.

Still, LSU—ahead 12-10—got another shot to put the game away when Allen fumbled at the USC 22 and Tiger nose guard George Atiyeh recovered.

The opportunity was a disaster. On a dipsy-doodle incompletion, LSU was assessed a 15-yard penalty for offensive interference. Woodley lost two yards, the Tigers were called for delay of game, before Woodley lost six more. LSU ended up punting from its own 44—34 yards further from the Trojan goal than when it got the ball.

The sequence was crucial. Essentially, with its last shot at getting out of Tiger Stadium with a victory, USC started a do-or-die drive.

* * *

Three plays later, on [third-and-9] from the USC 36 with three minutes to go, came the unkindest cut of all. McDonald called a pass play, but his line jumped before the snap. As Thibodeaux and Demetri Williams zeroed in on McDonald, he intentionally threw the ball away to avoid the very real possibility of a sack. A penalty flag fluttered to the

Tiger Stadium turf, and it seemed that everything was over except the shouting.

Then, incredibly, umpire Neil Gareb of the Pac-10 signalled a penalty against LSU!

Thibodeaux's hand brushed McDonald's helmet as he made the tackle. "When I reached out to grab him," Thibodeaux said, "his head moved, and my hand grazed his facemask."

Dismissing the offsides—then the intentional-grounding infraction—killed LSU's chances of offsetting penalties. The Tigers sagged almost visibly. They were able to slow the Trojan express just enough to force another third down, at the LSU-8. McDonald then hit 5-foot, 8-inch jitterbug Kevin Williams slicing across the middle for the touchdown on that play with 32 seconds left.

Yet, Ensminger very nearly pulled off a miracle on the second-to-last play, arcing a 30-yard rainbow to a streaking Willie Turner in the end zone. The ball fell though Turner's hands as he tried to make the catch and stay in bounds at the back line of the end zone.

The quest was over, but LSU had no reason to hang its head.

"When you look at our team compared to theirs," McClendon mused afterward, "one-on-one, or even 11-on-11, the differences are obvious. But when you put a team before a crowd like tonight's, in a game like this, then that team must be measured from here," he said, pointing to his chest. "When a team plays with its heart, then the measuring stick between one team and another shortens."

* * *

LSU football made John Ed Bradley what he is today—literally.

Growing up the son of a football coach in Opelousas, Louisiana, the most vivid memories he has of his youngest days is the family of seven sitting outside on the patio barbecueing on Saturday nights, listening to Tiger radio broadcasts, his dad with a purple-and-gold cap tipped back on his head. The kids, dressed in their LSU uniforms, would act out the big plays, pretending to be this Tiger or that, until his dad would sit John Ed next to him and say, "Settle down, now. LSU's on."

Against "The Next Generation" of athlete, John Ed Bradley more
than held his own.

"I think I was groomed to be an LSU Tiger," Bradley says now. An All-State lineman, Bradley had the size at 6 feet, 3 inches, and 215 pounds—and smarts—to go almost anywhere. Schools like Texas, Tulane, and Air Force were flooding his mailbox extolling their interest, not to mention the usual state schools like Louisiana Tech and Southwestern Louisiana.

Everyone, it seemed, wanted Bradley but LSU.

"They came in late," he said. "They didn't really recruit me. My first inkling that LSU might want me was going to my locker after a game, starting to pull my jersey off and behind me came three LSU coaches, with Jerry Stovall in the middle. He was still a golden name from the past, and the first thing he said to me was 'We want you at LSU.' And I answered, 'Coach, I'm coming. Tell me where and when to report.'"

Combining football and classwork, though, is different in high school and college. Bradley intended to major in zoology and eventually to go medical school. But he started having problems with science courses because of the amount of time required for football.

"My grades started falling," he said. Always an exceptional English student, Bradley started taking more and writing courses to boost his grade-point-average. After a couple of semesters, with his grades improving and him getting strong encouragement from some of his professors who felt he had a natural talent—not to mention Bradley says he was bitten deep by the writing-bug—he turned his complete attention to polishing his writing skills.

Just out of college, Ben Bradlee of *The Washington Post* hired him, and a few years later, his first novel, *Tupelo Nights*, was published. Between novels, Bradley works as a special contributor to *Sports Illustrated*.

* * *

That game showed Bradley's biggest critic, himself, exactly what he was capable of on the football field. The grade for a good game, or slightly above that, for an offensive lineman was in the 80s. In the one game he'll never forget, in the one game in which he played every offensive snap, including extra-point and field-goal attempts and deep snapping on punts, Bradley received a 92—almost the equivalent of a commendation in McClendon's rating system—and the highest of any offensive player that night.

And, it was also one of those you're-never-too-old-to-learn moments. Bradley was a college senior and had been playing football for well more than 10 years.

"But I learned something that night," he said with a sigh that echoed across two decades. "I never believed that one play, one call, one call ever really changed the outcome of a game.

"That night I learned better."

CHAPTER 4

BILLY
CANNON

LSU 7 - Ole Miss 3
October 31, 1959 • Tiger Stadium

The moment could be a metaphor for Billy Cannon's life: Richard Nixon, then the vice-president of the United States, was presenting Cannon the highest individual award in college football, the Heisman Trophy. Nixon misjudged the weight of the 50-pound bronze statue and almost dropped it. Lunging for it, Cannon saved the day—and the statue.

Cannon was almost always there when he was needed most. That's why from the mid-1950s, when he burst into the consciousness of Louisiana sports fans, up to today, in some quarters he is almost a folkhero, one of the most revered sports figures in state history.

On the other hand, to others who say he fumbled his legacy and brought shame to LSU, Cannon is one of Louisiana's most reviled figures.

There was no question, though, that in the age when Ike was president and Elvis was king—particularly in 1959 and perhaps for a season or two before that, Cannon was the nation's best collegiate player. A 6-foot, 1-inch, 210-pound halfback with Olympic sprinter speed and an Olympic-caliber weightlifter, he received 1,929 Heisman votes, more than tripling the total of the runner-up, Richie Lucas of Penn State; and Cannon's total was more than the combined vote of the next eight contenders.

As the spearhead of LSU's undefeated national championship team, Cannon was loved and admired in Louisiana. In the Tigers' illustrious football history, a span covering more than a century, his No. 20 is the only football jersey ever retired by the school.

But all that changed in 1983 when Cannon, an orthodontist in Baton Rouge, was caught in a counterfeiting scheme, embarrassing—even mortifying—those who had applauded him loudest. Long after serving two and a half years in prison, Cannon has made a comeback of sorts. Just as he saved Nixon's fumble in 1959, Cannon, who now works on prisoners' teeth at Angola, the Louisiana state prison—a calling he says was "inspired"—may have recovered his self-respect.

* * *

It's still seen every Halloween on grainy black-and-white film on television sets across Louisiana: Billy Cannon's almost superhuman run to football immortality. Then, as now, it was almost surreal: Cannon galloping like the Headless Horseman riding through Sleepy Hollow, but this time, eerily and bewitchingly, across Death Valley.

LSU played its first football game in 1893; and no single other play in all that time comes close to Cannon's in drama, impact, and long-lasting influence.

To put the 1959 Ole Miss-LSU contest in perspective, both teams were undefeated with 6-0 records. LSU was ranked No. 1—had been since the week leading up to their game the year before—and Ole Miss ranked No. 3. Opponents had scored a combined total of just 13 points—two field goals against the Tigers, one touchdown against the Rebels—against these sturdy defenses. Decades later Johnny Vaught, the Rebels' coach, described them thusly: "Both LSU and Ole Miss had just about as good defensive units as college football has ever seen."

Cannon echoed those sentiments about his opponents, saying, "Ole Miss was as good a football team as could have been fielded in those days."

Interestingly, new and stronger floodlights had been installed in Tiger Stadium since the 1958 season. With the 100-percent humidity, according to the *Baton Rouge State-Times*, "The foggy field assumed an

Billy Cannon on his epic punt return in 7-3 victory in 1959 classic.

unearthly quality under those lights," which obviously added to the dramatic setting.

Cannon very nearly became the game's goat in the first quarter. Punting very effectively, Ole Miss bottled LSU up at its own 5-yard line. On a 10-yard gain, Cannon dropped the second of three first-half fumbles. Billy Brewer recovered on the 20, and in four plays Ole Miss was planted on the Tiger 4-yard line. Somehow, some way, the defense held, and Bob Khayat, later the chancellor at Ole Miss, kicked a field goal.

A 3-0 lead would have been enough for Ole Miss against most opponents. After gaining the advantage, and with the Tigers constantly playing in the shadows of their own goal, Rebel coach Johnny Vaught wanted LSU to handle the slippery ball. One lapse, one mistake, and he felt the Rebels could finish the kill.

A third-quarter Cannon interception got LSU onto the Ole Miss side of the field, but Wendell Harris—five for five in field-goal attempts going into the game—missed. Vaught's cat-and-mouse strategy had LSU on the ropes. By the fourth quarter the Tigers seemed worn and beaten for the first time in 18 games.

With 10 minutes remaining, though, Vaught's tactics blew up. Cannon drifted back to the LSU-5 to field Jake Gibbs' third-down punt, Ole Miss' most consistent and effective play of the night.

Cannon said his earlier fumble did not make him hesitant.

"I didn't let things like that affect me—you couldn't," he said, admitting what happened next was risky, but calculated. "We had a rule of not handling kicks inside the 15, but I had broke four tackles on a previous punt, although I didn't get much out of it, and it was getting late. I thought, 'If I see a chance I'm going to try to bring it back.'"

The ball bounced high, right into Cannon's arms at the 11. He was hit several yards upfield, shook off the tackle, and maintained his balance. Richard Price made a futile attempt at Cannon at the 19, and Jerry Daniels slipped off the now steaming Tiger runner. At the 25, a Rebel mob enclosed around Cannon, but in a millisecond, he came busting out. By the time he passed Vaught at midfield, eight Rebels had gotten at least a hand on Cannon, and only Gibbs, 10 yards straight ahead, still had an opportunity to stop him.

"I figured Jake was waiting on me to cut back on him," Cannon said, "so I gave him a little juke and went inside. ... I know people say you can't think like that during the heat of a game, but that's how I got past Gibbs."

Dan Hardesty of the *Baton Rouge State-Times* wrote of the hair-raising play that Cannon was like "a white-shirted ghost wearing jersey No. 20."

Tiger Stadium erupted with ear-splitting emotion, and Cannon was mobbed in the end zone by teammates—and others. "I was so tired I could barely stand," Cannon said. "After I gave the ball to the official, a guy in a red corduroy jacket came racing out of the stands. I had my hands on my knees, trying to catch my breath, and the fellow started pounding me, really clobbering me on the back, and I was too tired to stop him. Donnie Daye finally pulled him off me, and I don't know whether he'd just won a million dollars or lost a million dollars."

The suspense wasn't over, though. A silence crept over the stadium as more and more fans caught sight of a penalty flag near midfield. Finally, officials confirmed the touchdown. Ole Miss had been in motion on the punt. Harris' conversion made the score 7-3, LSU.

In a surprise move, Vaught inserted sophomore Doug Elmore at quarterback to pull the game out for the Rebels in the remaining 10 minutes. Starting at the Rebel 32, Elmore ignited a long, arduous march, flinging his backs against the famed Chinese Bandits and slowly worming into position for victory.

"I was getting oxygen on the sidelines, watching Doug pick up first down after first down," Cannon said. "I thought to myself, 'Here's the best run I ever made in my life, and we're going to lose.'"

When Ole Miss penetrated to the LSU-23, Coach Paul Dietzel took out the Chinese Bandits—his defensive specialists—and sent his front-line troops back in, though the advance continued. The drive reached the LSU-7 with 90 seconds left. In the three ensuing plays, Ole Miss worked itself to the LSU 2, forcing a win-or-lose, fourth-and-goal situation very reminiscent of the goal-line stand of 1958.

Elmore slammed off-tackle where Warren Rabb stopped his forward progress, and Cannon finished the tackle one yard short of the end zone. LSU regained possession with 18 seconds remaining.

Cannon was a hero on both offense and defense, but it was clearly the Herculean run—which has become the signature play of LSU football history—that was seared onto the memory banks of college fans. Johnny Vaught remembered it in his autobiography, *Rebel Coach*, as "… surely one of the greatest in the history of collegiate football. That boy could have gone down at least four times, but he simply wouldn't be headed."

Immediately after the game, a relieved Dietzel sighed, "That was the greatest run I ever saw in football."

Decades later, Dietzel said nothing he has seen since has changed his mind.

* * *

LSU didn't repeat as national champion. A fluky 14-13 upset loss to Tennessee the week after Ole Miss—a game in which both Cannon and Johnny Robinson each outgained the entire Volunteer team—finished off those aspirations.

Cannon was again a unanimous All-America selection, and, of course, the Heisman Trophy recipient. He had signed during the season with Pete Rozelle—then the general manager of the Los Angeles Rams of the National Football League—but then was lured to the Houston Oilers of the new American Football League with the first six-figure contract ever in pro football.

In 1960, Cannon was an All-Pro halfback and the MVP in the championship game as the Oilers won the AFL title. A year later, he was again an All-Pro after leading the AFL in rushing with 948 yards, and in one stunning performance accounted for 331 total yards (115 receiving) and five touchdowns against the New York Titans. He again was the AFL championship game MVP as the Oilers won the title a second straight time.

What seemed to be the start of a golden career, though, took a wicked twist in 1962 when a linebacker came down knees first on Cannon's back and tore his back muscles loose. Never possessed with great lateral movement, when Cannon tried to come back weeks later he had practically none.

Two years later Cannon was traded to the Oakland Raiders for three players, and he played the 1964 season at flanker. Oakland coach Al Davis asked Cannon to move to tight end in '65, where he played primarily as a backup for two years.

In 1967, though, Cannon caught fire—and footballs by the bushel—becoming a dangerous receiving threat in the Raiders' offensive scheme with 32 catches, 10 for touchdowns, as the Raiders made way to Super Bowl II. Cannon was an All-Pro selection once again.

"He was the classic case of too much too soon," Davis said at the time. "Money, fame, buildup. It came close to ruining him. The wolves [who] love to see a hero fail couldn't wait to jump on him. But he took his beating and came back and made good at a new position, and now he's the best tight end in the business."

Cannon spent nine off-seasons in his 11-year pro career studying denistry, and when he finished playing in 1970 with Hank Stram's Kansas City Chiefs, he returned to Baton Rouge where he opened what proved to be a thriving orthodontic practice. Cannon also built a reputation for treating children from families that couldn't always pay for the cost of dental care.

"I think maybe the biggest thrill I ever had," Cannon once said, "was receiving the high school graduation picture of a beautiful kid who used to be made fun of and called 'Fang,' but who now had a beautiful smile, with the words 'Thank you' written across it."

Still, there was some distance growing between Cannon and LSU, in part for his harsh public criticism of Tiger coach Charlie McClendon, and in part because his son, Billy Cannon Jr., chose to play football at Texas A&M. There was a general feeling among some of the LSU faithful that Cannon was no longer one of them, and, in some quarters, he was resented.

So the wolves that love to see a hero fail eventually had a feast upon Cannon's implication in the counterfeiting operation. At his sentencing in 1983, the only LSU person on hand was former sports information director Paul Manasseh, who said he felt someone from LSU should be at Cannon's side.

It didn't get much better two and a half years later when he was released. On his first day back at his orthodontic practice, a woman's

Billy Cannon steps through a cluster of Mississippi Rebels.

voice on Cannon's intercom began screeching, "Jailbird, jailbird, jailbird." Cannon, who was in the embarrassed company of well-wishers at the time, recalled saying, "I wonder if she thinks I don't know I was in jail."

Once on a radio talk show, one caller began shouting, "Dr. Cannon, you're a disgrace to LSU and to the Heisman Trophy!"

It began to get better. Former athletic director Joe Dean made an effort to bring Cannon back into the fold. "We like to think our people, LSU Tigers, are special," Dean said. "We all make mistakes, even those who like to point fingers at others. Billy Cannon is a special person. We want him here, with us."

While incarcerated, Cannon saw a need for his services, and now he works with the prisoners at Angola. He seems to have come to terms with his personal failures and successes. He does not flinch when he is reminded of his errors.

"I know who I am," he said, "what I did, and what I have to live with. I have my past to live with, and I realize that. You know the old story: You join a church, you're reborn, and your past is washed away. Well, that's not so. You live with your past.

"And I do."

CHAPTER 5

CARLOS
CARSON

LSU 77 - Rice 0
September 24, 1977 • Tiger Stadium

First, there was a 22-yard hook pass, which Carlos Carson caught for a touchdown.

Then there was a 29-yard streak play, which Carlos Carson caught for a touchdown.

Later there was a 63-yard bomb, which Carlos Carson caught for a touchdown.

Later still there was a 20-yard crossing pattern, which Carlos Carson caught for a touchdown.

Thankfully, there was a halftime to break the monotony.

But then came the third quarter—and yet another bomb, this one for 67 yards, which, you guessed it, Carlos Carson caught for a touchdown.

This was clearly a night to remember.

"In all the years since then," Carson said, "that game has never really left my mind."

It's always there, sitting there just beyond his consciousness, ready for easy discussion—and with good reason.

With five touchdown receptions, Carlos Carson had a night to remember.

Carson had a game like no Tiger—maybe like no player anywhere—ever had: he touched the ball five times and scored five touchdowns. He broke the NCAA record for most consecutive touchdown passes caught and Southeastern Conference records for most touchdowns in a game and most average yards per catch, 40.2. Carson's five receptions covered 201 yards.

"It seemed like [quarterbacks] Steve [Ensminger] and David [Woodley] were perfect," Carson recalled, "and everything I got my hands on just stuck to my fingers."

The statement was reflected elsewhere in the record book, too. Ensminger's four touchdown passes set the LSU record, and the 77-0 score represented the Tigers' highest point total in 41 seasons.

After the 11-touchdown debacle against the Owls, LSU receivers coach Jim Collier sighed, "Tonight, [Carson] and the quarterbacks did something I've never seen before—long passing in which not one of the receivers ever had to hesitate, jump up, or wait for a pass."

The display was amazing, even if against a hapless Rice squad. The most surprising thing about that night, though, was not the records or the score—Carson, then an 18-year-old sophomore split end starting his first game in Tiger Stadium, had never before made a catch as a collegian.

"I called my parents afterward to tell them," Carson said. "They had already heard it on the news. But I didn't know I had set all those records for a couple of days."

It was surprising not only because of the obvious. LSU under Coach Charlie McClendon had a run-first-and-foremost mentality, and, indeed, the Tigers didn't ignore that phase of the game against the Owls. Tailback Charles Alexander gained 155 yards of LSU's 502 rushing yards.

"Charles would soften up anybody's line," Carson said admiringly even decades later. "He did that night, too, but for whatever reason, the coaches also kept calling pass plays, which is not what they usually tended to call. They kept calling my number all night, it seemed like. I loved it."

* * *

The long-shot circumstances that brought Carson to Tiger Stadium bewilder even him. The LSU coaching staff wasn't hot on his trail. No one was. A fullback on the J.I. Leonard High School in West Palm Beach, Florida was the guy Tiger coaches had their eyes on. But it was hard concentrating on that prospect while analyzing him on film. Another back kept breaking their collective concentration, doing one thing or another that caught their attention. It didn't take long to realize that the halfback who kept diverting their attention was as good an athlete as anyone else LSU was recruiting.

"I immediately got on the phone to the high school coach and asked him about the halfback," Tiger assistant Scooter Purvis said. "He told me he couldn't believe it, but there wasn't one school in the country after him. No one wanted him."

At the moment, Carson's college athletic possibilities seemed to consist of attending Florida A&M and trying out for the track team— or picking out a major school where he could try to make the football team as a walk-on.

Purvis hopped a plane to West Palm Beach, where Carson and his parents awaited his arrival.

Carson was everything the coach wanted him to be, as an athlete, a student, and a person. He was a little on the light side, 5 feet, 11 inches, 167 pounds, but was a sprinter whose personal best was a 9.5 in the 100-yard dash but who hit 9.7 with consistency.

Purvis decided he wanted Carson and started to broach the subject of a visit to LSU. "I began hinting around, during our talk, about nothing more than a visit to the campus, and Carlos said straight out, 'Coach, are you offering me a scholarship?' I said, 'Yes' and he said, 'I accept.'"

Carson officially became an LSU athlete without ever seeing the Tiger campus—and "athlete" was the precise word because his days in the backfield were finished. He and the coaches were fully aware of it, and not just because of Alexander's presence.

"I knew I was too light," Carson said. "I knew I was going to have to play another position."

He was turned into a split end, which was not a headline position in that run-oriented offense, but Carson would lead the Tigers in

Carlos Carson (3) celebrates one of his five touchdowns against Rice.

receiving in two of his three varsity seasons, accounting for 1,728 career yards and 14 touchdowns.

* * *

LSU needed a victory—and wanted a measuring stick—when it played its first 1977 home game against Rice.

The Tigers opened the season as 24-21 upset victims at Indiana, while the Owls entered Tiger Stadium with a 1-1 record, having lost the previous week to Florida, LSU's next opponent.

"We were coming off a bad game at Indiana," Carson remembered. "Even though it was early in the season, we felt we had to play well."

Right off the bat, Carson was LSU's go-to guy.

"I turned around [in the end zone], and there was the ball," he said. "I went, 'Wow, this isn't bad.' It turned out to be one of those magic nights in Tiger Stadium."

The passes kept coming, and Carson kept catching them. "I didn't know why, but the coaches kept calling passes for me. I just did what we'd been practicing for a month—just more of it."

It was an unusual game plan for the Tigers. Apparently, McClendon decided to teach the Owls a lesson for not respecting LSU's pass-play capability.

"We called the passes from the sidelines," Charlie Mac said after a game in which the Tigers rolled up a total of 244 yards on their seven receptions. "We noticed the corner playing up too close, and we just let [Carson] roll."

Still, once things started getting out of hand, McClendon tried to call off the dogs against the Owls, clearing his bench and playing all 65 of his players.

"But," Carson said, "I think we may have shown people that we could pass."

Indeed. In fact, Carson's history-making trek continued. The following week, in a 36-14 defeat of Florida, Carson caught the first pass thrown his way for a 15-yard touchdown—making it six consecutive receptions for six touchdowns—an NCAA record which still stands—and a moment Carson savored.

"Yes," he said. "That was my home-state team, and Florida didn't recruit me. In fact, they didn't recruit anybody from West Palm Beach from my time there. I enjoyed leaving a mark on Florida."

Through all the ensuing years, that Rice game—the very epitome of a "Game of a Lifetime"—has stayed with Carson.

"That game," he said with a laugh, "is really a big part of me. Anyone from LSU hears my name, and they think of that night. I think of LSU, and I remember it, too."

* * *

A notable pro career with the Kansas City Chiefs ensued, and Carson left a quiet but deep imprint on the NFL.

He played 12 years with the Chiefs, setting a team record with 80 receptions in 1983, when he also led the NFL in receiving yards (1,351). Another 1,000-plus-yard season followed in '84. In 1988, he was named to the Pro Bowl squad.

Carson, who owns two fast-food franchises in the Kansas City area, is still second in Chiefs annals with 18 games of 100 or more receiving yards, trailing only Hall of Famer Otis Taylor.

CHAPTER 6

TOMMY CASANOVA

LSU 61 - Ole Miss 17
December 5, 1970 • Tiger Stadium

The blue-shirted Rebels were bearing down on him, and, through the tintinnabulation of Tiger Stadium, Tommy Casanova heard the yells of a teammate for him to fair catch the punt.

But he didn't.

Deciding to take the chance, Casanova gathered the ball in, stepped into and then out of the initial wave of Rebels, picked up his blockers, faked out one last defender, and then glided into the end zone.

"That was it, the play that broke our backs," Ole Miss superstar Archie Manning said decades later. The 61-yard return put LSU ahead 21-10 with 3:58 remaining in the first half, breathing room against an opponent—and a quarterback—who broke Tiger hearts and aspirations the frustrating two previous seasons. It brought a barrage of oranges from the stands, a game-long if not very original signal of LSU's next stop with the victory: the Orange Bowl.

But there was more to come—much more.

"Caz" returned another punt 76 yards for a fourth-quarter touchdown, tying the NCAA individual record for a single game. Teammate Craig Burns ran back a third kick 61 yards as LSU tied the NCAA team record for punts run back for touchdowns.

The Tigers intercepted five Ole Miss passes—one by Casanova, three by Burns—and ran up an astounding 811 all-purpose yards (306 in return yardage) as both the offense and defense outplayed and outscored Ole Miss in every phase.

In the most lopsided margin in the series between these two ancient rivals, the Rebels could garner only 62 rushing yards. Manning completed 12 of his 22 throws but was intercepted twice and left the game with minus-25 yards on the ground.

"There's no way we were that much better than Ole Miss," Casanova reflected. "It was just one of those games where things just started rolling our way and never stopped. It was just our night."

A night two long years overdue, according to Tiger fans.

* * *

Manning, even then, before his college career was over, was being called, by some, "the best quarterback ever to play in the SEC," a league with a quarterback-rich heritage.

No one would get an argument from the Tigers, who lost two straight—along with an undefeated 1969 season and the league title—to the improbable but very real heroics of the red-haired Mississippian with Huckleberry Finn looks. They played an emotional role in the run-up to the game.

There were a dozen storylines between the Rebels—7-2 entering the game—and the 8-2 Bayou Bengals.

It was an odd season finale. Prior to the season, the schools agreed to reschedule their game to the end of the season for national television, pushing the end of the regular season back a week.

- LSU had to win to go to the Orange Bowl. The invitation was extended on the proviso the Tigers prevailed in their last two games against Tulane and Ole Miss. The Tigers trounced Tulane, and now they had to beat the Rebels. The other bowls were set. There were no other options for LSU. It was the Orange Bowl or nothing.
- Manning suffered a fractured arm against Houston on November 7, ending his Heisman hopes, but he was determined to return against LSU and play with a protective pad on his left arm.

- Rebel coach Johnny Vaught suffered a mild heart attack midway through the season, and assistant Bruiser Kinard took over for the last four games of the season.
- And, oh, yes, of major importance, with a victory—and LSU had not beaten Ole Miss in five years—the Tigers would claim the league title.

"We were pretty fragile," Manning said, "a quarterback with a broken arm and a coach who had a heart attack. "We hoped maybe things would break for us, and we'd get lucky and maybe find a way to beat LSU again. We played with a lot of emotion, and it carried us for a while."

The Tigers played with emotion, too, perhaps remembering 1969—and the overhead sign on the tunnel entrance as they filed through on their way to the field: "SEC Champs? It's up to you to remove the question mark."

It took a little while—with LSU losing three early fumbles, Manning put Ole Miss ahead 7-0 in the first quarter—but the Tigers nudged ahead. Then, after Casanova's derring-do on the first punt return, the Bengals blew it open.

* * *

"We knew with Archie, the great competitor that he is, trying to come back, that they'd be fired up," Casanova said. "The thing is, it got us fired up too."

With very good reason:

Manning bedeviled a pair of very good LSU teams—the 1969 Tigers being perhaps the school's best with an offense that averaged 35 points a game and a defense that surrendered just 384 rushing yards all season. As a sophomore in 1968, Manning completed 24-of-40 passes for 345 yards, passing for two touchdowns and running for a third, rallying the Rebels from a 17-3 deficit to a 27-24 victory, the winning TD pass coming in the fading seconds. As a junior, he was 22-of-36 for 210 yards, passing for one touchdown, running for three, plus a two-point conversion in overcoming a 23-12 third-quarter LSU lead for a 26-23 upset that cost the Tigers the SEC title and the possibility of a shot

Tommy Casanova was one of the most versatile Tigers ever.

at the national championship. Combined, it meant Manning riddled the defenses of two very good LSU defensive units for 555 yards in eight quarters, during which he accounted for all of his team's touchdowns. To put what Manning did to LSU in perspective, consider that, after he ran for three touchdowns against the Tigers in 1969, LSU went its next 12 games without permitting a single rushing touchdown.

Beating a less-than-100-percent Manning couldn't, in fact, possibly deliver the maximum sense of satisfaction. ... But it was still pretty sweet. Perhaps the loudest reaction of 1970 in Louisiana came when, minutes after Casanova's return, lineman Ronnie Estay tackled the Tiger nemesis in the end zone for a safety.

* * *

There's a mutual admiration society among elite athletes—especially these two, who are enshrined in the College Football Hall of Fame. Manning said of Casanova, whom he played against both in college and the NFL, "The only thing better than Tommy as a football player is Tommy as a human being. He ranked in the handful of best defensive backs in college, where I saw him most; and probably could have played any position on his team, and played it well."

Truly. A three-time All-America defensive back at LSU and an All-Pro safety with the Cincinnati Bengals, Casanova was one of the most complete athletes ever to play in Louisiana.

A pro scout said after watching Casanova at practice at LSU, "My wife could scout Tommy and put him down as a first-round draft choice."

To put Casanova, who was recruited by only three universities, into the context of LSU football, when fans were asked to vote on a modern-era LSU all-century team Casanova received more votes than any other Tiger.

"Aw, that's ridiculous," Casanova responded at the news. But was it?

In today's game of specialization, he was so good that Tiger coaches didn't know what to do with him. As a sophomore and junior, he played both offense and defense; and the dark-haired Casanova, with looks to match his name, gained 302 yards rushing in spot duty on offense,

Two punt returns for touchdowns by Tommy Casanova ignited a rout.

returned punts for 491 yards, returned kickoffs for 334 yards, intercepted seven passes and shut down numerous receivers—always drawing the ace of the opposing team.

An athlete of infinite grace, on the gridiron Casanova was reminiscent of a dancer on stage. "He was tremendously gifted," said Charlie McClendon, the Tiger coach, "one of the most gifted athletes I ever had. There's no question he could have been an All-America running back and really could have jazzed up our offense; but I needed him more on defense."

Casanova's sheer presence diverted opponents' passing schemes to other parts of the field, and thanks to other superb defenders, such as linebacker Mike Anderson and tackle Ronnie Estay, McClendon's defense led the nation in 1970 by yielding the minuscule scoring average of 8.7 points a game.

It was that kind of performance that caught the eye of *Sports Illustrated*, which made Casanova its cover boy for the 1971 college football issue, proclaiming him the nation's most complete football player.

"I don't look back and think of 'high points,' per se," Casanova, now an ophthalmologist in his hometown of Crowley, Louisiana, said. "Most of my games sort of blend together. The Auburn game [a 21-20 LSU victory] my sophomore year would rank with my most vivid memories. Auburn had [quarterback Pat] Sullivan and [receiver Terry] Beasley, and they were definitely a Top 10 team."

In that game, Casanova made a brilliant tackle behind the line on a fourth-down play inside the LSU 5. He dismisses the play "… because we knew what was coming. Auburn was very well scouted. Too much was made of that tackle."

Not to anyone in the stands, it wasn't—nor to the national television audience.

None of that compares to the most difficult thing Casanova ever had to overcome—combining medical school with his pro career in Cincinnati.

"That really became rough," he said. "I wouldn't want to do that again. In fact, if I had to do it again now, I don't think I'd try it. I'd choose one over the other, but I'm not sure which one it would be."

* * *

"The funny thing is," Dr. Casanova said, "I really always played football for the fun of it. I'm far more competitive now. I coach my little boy in peewee games, and, of course, you want the kids to have the best experience. That means they have to win some, and looking out for them in that regard brings out the competitive juices in me. It's just now that I'm beginning to realize what Coach Mac must've been going through with us."

Maybe, maybe not.

"I felt we had the weight of the stadium on us," said McClendon after the Rebel victory, thinking back on how close his team had come to a 10-0-1 regular season. The Tigers dropped a 20-18 decision on a last-second fluke to Texas A&M in the season opener, and lost 3-0 to Notre Dame in South Bend, the field goal coming after Casanova, of all people, dropped an interception in the end zone.

On the other hand, Casanova did help the Tigers emphatically erase the question mark on the sign above their tunnel entrance.

CHAPTER 7

ROHAN DAVEY

LSU 28 - Georgia Tech 14
December 29, 2000 • Atlanta, Georgia

Peering intently into the faces of his teammates, Rohan Davey said simply: "We're going to win this game!"

Big words for a quarterback whose team was down 14-3 at the half; for a quarterback whose offense barely managed a moribund 117 yards in the opening 30 minutes of the Peach Bowl; for a quarterback who hadn't taken a snap in five-and-a-half games—22 complete quarters to be precise.

In the locker room of the Georgia Dome, Coach Nick Saban told Davey to get ready. He was starting the second half of a game that had all the earmarks of a lost cause. He replaced Josh Booty, who had labored vainly against an intense and focused Georgia Tech defense that limited him to eight completions in 19 attempts for 110 yards, sacked him three times, and hurried him on practically every throw, including screen passes. The Tiger rushing game amassed all of seven yards on 18 carries.

"Surprised might not be the right word," Davey recalled. "I was more than just surprised. Coach didn't like changing quarterbacks, and that wasn't the first time we got off to a slow start; so, no, I wasn't even thinking I might be going in."

Then Saban said, essentially, "You're on!"

That may have been the upset of LSU's season considering Davey hadn't been on the field for so long, and Booty had already been selected as the All-SEC quarterback by the league coaches.

Davey was, however, more than up to the task at hand.

"He comes in the huddle in the third quarter, and it was like turning on a light switch," safety Ryan Clark marveled.

Suddenly the Tiger offense lurched into high gear. Davey moved LSU 70 yards in nine plays, completing five passes in five attempts, covering 57 yards—the last one to fullback Tommy Banks for three yards and a touchdown. The seemingly almost-forgotten backup had breathed life into the listless Tigers.

LSU changed its mode of operation to a quick-strike passing offense, but Davey's presence—and that of usual starter at offensive tackle Brandon Winey, who was out with a broken wrist in the first quarter but suited up and rushed in to help his mates—lifted the spirits of the Tigers, who demonstrably were playing harder. The rise in morale spread to the defensive unit that had been ripped for 150 first-half rushing yards. Now it was stopping Tech cold, forcing turnovers and making the Yellow Jackets punt when they did hold onto the ball, all giving Davey more opportunities to make impact plays. Quickly releasing the ball, Davey was burning Tech outside and down the middle, and when he was about to go under the rush, he found ways to step out of trouble and tackles and move the chains.

Davey literally took over the game.

Three possessions after LSU's first touchdown, Davey, a quarterback with the size of a linebacker, 6-feet-3, 239 pounds—took the Bayou Bengals on another drive. This one went 53 yards, and he was three-for-four for 26 yards, the payoff being the defining play of the day in sequence. On third-and-goal strike from the Tech 9, Davey bought some time, then speared Josh Reed, leaping near the back end of the end zone and coming down with just inches to spare. The play put the Tigers ahead for good.

There was more to come.

LSU went for its second two-point conversion again, and Tech put on a heavy—and seemingly effective—blitz. The 'Jackets reached Davey,

Coming off the bench, Rohan Davey lifted the Tigers.

and spun him around. On his way down, he spotted Reed once more and got off a perfect pass.

"That throw tells you what Rohan is all about," LSU linebacker Trev Faulk said at the time. "After he comes up with a play like that, there was no way we were going to lose."

Of course, that was true. Davey finished 17-of-25 for 174 yards and three touchdowns in his 30 minutes of play, and LSU had its come-from-behind victory. Davey brought something with him when he took the field, and it wasn't just physical talent.

"With Rohan, we were able to go to our quick passing game and do more play-action faking," offensive coordinator Jimbo Fisher said. "Most of the time, Josh made the right reads, but we just couldn't give him any protection. Josh wasn't playing that poorly. We just, as a team, weren't playing that well," Fisher reflected. "What we needed was an emotional lift, and Ro was our emotional leader."

* * *

Davey, who has spent the last few years in the NFL and backed up Tom Brady on three Super Bowl teams with the New England Patriots, thought back on the 2000 Peach Bowl and said it was the most important game he played in college.

That's saying a lot because Davey was the SEC player of the week after a scintillating season-ending performance against Arkansas in 1999, and he was the national player of the week after quarterbacking the Tigers to an overtime victory over Tennessee in 2000, and also after an electrifying game against Alabama in 2001. In the turnaround regular-season game of the 2001 season, which ended with an SEC championship for LSU, Davey did what no quarterback had ever done at LSU, or what no quarterback anywhere had ever done to 'Bama: he passed for 528 yards in a 35-21 Tiger victory. He followed that up with an MVP performance in the Sugar Bowl, where he set records for completions (31-of-41) and yardage (444) in a 47-34 win against Illinois.

"Yes, I've was in some memorable games at LSU," he reflected with obvious pride. "The Peach Bowl, though, to me was the one I put at the top of the list because without it some of the others might not have ever happened. It opened the gates for me."

* * *

Coach Gerry DiNardo hit a quarterback motherlode in 1998 when he successfully reeled in prize recruit Craig Nall of Alexandria, Lousiana, then fell into Josh Booty—who was the bluest of blue chip prep quarterbacks in 1993, when he came out of Shreveport's Evangel Christian Academy. None other than Bill Walsh, then the reigning genius of NFL football, said Booty was "… the best high school quarterback I've ever seen." That was quite a mouthful considering Booty was a senior the same year as fellow Louisianian Peyton Manning.

After graduation, five years later, Booty opted to take his athletic talents to baseball, signing a baseball-only contract as the Florida Marlins' first-round pick in 1994. But baseball didn't work out, and Booty left to try to achieve his boyhood dream: to quarterback the LSU Tigers.

Then one of the nation's target recruits, Davey, chose LSU over West Virginia, Tennessee, Notre Dame, and his hometown Miami Hurricanes, setting off a roller-coaster tenure in Baton Rouge.

"The fans sold me," he said. "I loved the LSU fans, their enthusiasm, their loyalty. They were fun to be around, pleasant, and they could energize you. I've never regretted that decision."

Not even with two other major quarterback talents (and they would all put in time in the NFL) with whom to compete.

There would be a lot of frustration—and a keen sense of betrayal—before a happy ending.

* * *

The three-man quarterback derby was the talk of Louisiana leading up to the 1999 season, and DiNardo couldn't seem to separate the troika.

On "a gut feeling," Nall started the opener against San Jose State, with Davey playing the second half and the first half of the second game against North Texas.

Then the tough times really started. In a disaster against Auburn, in LSU's SEC opener, Davey was 4-for-11 with two interceptions before being benched in favor of Booty. And that was almost the end of Davey.

Despite the fact that Booty was struggling almost as bad as Davey did as LSU went on an eight-game losing skein, in the period between Auburn and the season-ending game with Arkansas, Davey threw a grand total of 13 passes.

Then DiNardo was fired with a game remaining and interim coach Hal Hunter started Davey. He responded by completing 10-of-12 passes for 224 yards and three touchdowns in the Tigers' 35-10 victory, LSU's lone SEC victory.

That night Davey was eating out with friends when one received a cell-phone call. It was from DiNardo, who wanted to congratulate Davey on his performance.

Davey refused to take the call.

* * *

Still, life didn't get any easier. That February, Davey tore the anterior cruciate ligament in his left leg while warming up for, of all things, a charity basketball game.

That meant while his quarterback rivals were absorbing a new system under new coach Nick Saban, Davey was undergoing rigorous rehabilitation. Following surgery, while Booty and Nall were taking snaps in spring practice, Davey tried to soak up the new system at the same time he was spending five hours a day strengthening the injured knee.

Of course, physically, he was far behind the others. It was up to Fisher, asked to rate the three in spring practice, who put his finger on the pulse of the situation. "All three are very gifted," Fisher said. "They have the physical talents ... but that does not make you a quarterback. You've got to have 'It'—that persona where you can't help but be successful."

"It" was in Davey's DNA, but trying to beat out Booty would be a mighty task.

Booty, though, opened the door for Davey in the fourth week of the season with a bad decision leading to an embarrassing 13-10 upset to Alabama-Birmingham.

The next week against Tennessee, because of Booty's bruised ribs, Davey got the start. He responded by passing for four touchdowns and 318 yards in a 38-31 Tiger victory in overtime, but at a cost. The Vols knocked Davey all over Tiger Stadium, causing him to limp noticeably through the fourth quarter and overtime.

"He played with the heart of a lion out there," Saban said. " ... Ro had a big win and he deserves the opportunity to continue to lead the offense."

You know the saying: Be careful what you wish for.

A week later, at Florida, standing in a walking boot on his left foot to keep pressure off an ankle that was worse than when he sprained it against the Vols, Davey was a sitting duck.

That was the last time Davey would play in more than a month.

The intangibles Davey brought to his team, though, should have been evident after the season. Two weeks after the Tigers concluded their 7-4 regular-season, his teammates voted Davey, a junior, their permanent offensive captain.

"I wasn't surprised, because I know the kind of inspiration Rohan brought to our team," Saban said. "It wasn't the first time an underclassman [of Saban's] was a tri-captain, but I've never had a team when the honor went to a backup."

That fealty to their inspirational leader would pay off in 2001— after Davey showed what could be done in the second half of the Peach Bowl.

Things evened out after that, with Nall transferring and Booty taking off for the NFL.

Talking about that game still brings joy to Davey. "It may not have been my greatest game, but it was my greatest moment," he reiterated.

A strong statement, to be sure. After all, Davey left LSU as the only Tiger quarterback to throw for more than 3,000 yards, and the only one to pass for more than 300 yards in three straight games—though it certainly was a moment to remember.

Rohan Davey overcame adversity for a memorable career.

The veteran Fisher was moved while watching Davey run along the Georgia Dome end zone after the comeback against Georgia Tech, reaching up into the stands to slap hands with the sea of fans wearing purple-and-gold regalia.

"Just look at that," Fisher said at the time. "There's a kid with guts, without a selfish bone in his body. He's the kind a team feeds off. He's what the game is all about."

CHAPTER 8

WENDELL DAVIS

LSU 30 - South Carolina 13
December 31, 1987 • Jacksonville, Florida

Slicing toward the sideline, Wendell Davis looked back.

He saw the South Carolina defense swarming into the LSU backfield, but also saw that quarterback Tom Hodson had gotten off the pass, which was coming toward him.

Davis made the catch, stepped out of an attempted tackle by cornerback Robert Robinson at the 25, faked out another defender at the 20, picked up a block by teammate Tony Moss at the 10, and scooted into the end zone.

That 39-yard touchdown came on the Tigers' second play from scrimmage.

Three minutes later, LSU again beat the Gamecock blitz, and Davis again beat Robinson, making an above-the-head reception.

That 12-yard pass, coming with 10 minutes to play in the opening quarter of the '87 Gator Bowl, was LSU's fifth play—and second touchdown.

"I just missed a tackle on the first one and on the second, I was in position; but it was a great throw and catch," Robinson said. "You've got to give them credit. We were there, they just made the play."

And they continued to make plays all game long.

Davis scored a third touchdown on a 25-yard reception on LSU's first possession of the second half. "He just had everyone beat on that one," Hodson said. "Most of our routes are good against man-to-man. We have a great receiver, and he just beat them all night."

Indeed. Davis, the MVP in his farewell game at LSU, finished the Gator Bowl with nine receptions for 132 yards and his three touchdowns. He thought back to the decisive victory and reflected, "It was a great way to bow out."

* * *

Almost two decades after the fact, Davis still relishes the win. "It was sweet," Davis said with enthusiasm. "South Carolina was so incredibly cock-sure of themselves. For two weeks before the game, all we heard about was how good they were, from the media and from the Gamecocks themselves. It all kind of got us fired-up and ready to play."

South Carolina was kind of the flavor-of-the-month in college football, sort of a trendy team that wasn't usually found among the elite of the sport but with eye-catching success this season under former New York Giants coach Joe Morrison. Still, there wasn't enough difference between the Gator Bowl opponents to warrant an almost haughty attitude by Carolina.

After all, LSU was 9-1-1 entering their game, the Gamecocks were 8-3; LSU was ranked seventh. South Carolina was ranked ninth.

Yet, for the first time all season, LSU was an underdog. The Gamecocks were the four-point favorite.

The wide difference of perception between the teams was apparently based on an accomplished defense with a colorful nickname that could have been coined by Edgar Allen Poe: "The Black Death."

Highly respected and much-traveled coordinator Joe Lee Dunn molded Carolina's 50 defense into an all-out assault, blitzing relentlessly from all sides of the formation, sending a minimum of one defender and as many as eight into their opponent's backfield.

And with success. South Carolina went into the Gator Bowl second in the nation in scoring defense (10.1 points per game); third in total defense (227 yards); fifth in rushing defense (94 yards); and sixth in pass

Wendell Davis makes another of his patented catches.

defense (133 yards). Black Death averaged a sack for every 12 passing attempts—29 for the season—and forced 23 interceptions.

"Of course they were good, and we knew they were good," Davis said. "But, in case we didn't, they kept reminding us."

Gamecocks safety Greg Philpot said before the game: "If you beat us, you must beat the blitz. I don't think [LSU] can do it."

Carolina linebacker Matt McKernan said: "They know we're coming, but so did everyone else. Eight teams knew what we were going to do, but they still couldn't do anything about it. LSU is going to be very surprised at what we've got in store."

Cornerback Norman Floyd said: "They've done well protecting [quarterback Tom Hodson], but I don't think they'll be ready for what we've got."

Carolina, however, apparently did not have everything figured. Throughout the season the Tigers had handled the blitz well, allowing just nine sacks. And they had the weapons that could make a blitzing team pay, having totaled a school-record 4,843 yards of offense.

Wendell Davis, who finished the '87 season with 72 receptions, and who had set the LSU record of 80 as a junior, was one of the Tigers' prime offensive weapons.

* * *

It's funny how life turns out. Davis caught 183 passes in his LSU career, led the nation in receiving once with those 80 catches, and in the same season led the nation in touchdown receptions (11).

Every one of those—and what was then his school-record 19 career touchdown catches—may have been caused by nothing more than irregular yard lining in Tiger Stadium.

Until 1985 there was almost no running room outside the north end zone. A player ran out of that end line directly into a fence. The south end zone, on the other hand, had several yards of cushion between the end marker and fence.

On such miscalculations are All-Americans made.

The field was altered in '85, with the north end zone being moved out five yards. But before it was done, Glenn Holt, an up-and-coming

LSU receiver, shot into the north end zone during spring training to make a catch. He made the reception near the end marker and, moving at full speed, couldn't stop himself from slamming into the fence.

Holt put out his hand to break the momentum, breaking that hand.

The Tiger Stadium dimensions were adjusted shortly afterward, but the north end zone had claimed a victim. A bad break for Holt turned into the break of a lifetime for Davis.

Davis, Holt's best friend and a second-string flanker who caught exactly zero passes as a freshman, was switched to split end. Holt never could win back his job, took ill, and eventually left LSU.

Davis caught 31 passes as a sophomore before fully blossoming in his final two seasons, and he was recognized as a consensus All-American in his last year.

The absence of Holt combined with Wendell's rapid improvement turned Davis into Hodson's go-to guy. Though they only played together two years, Davis and Hodson forever became linked in LSU's collective memory bank.

But, interestingly, while Davis became the object of multiple coverage—and media coverage as a hot story—Glenn Holt faded from LSU memory. During the spring of 1987, two years after Holt's ill-fated crash into the north end zone fence, Davis turned a corner in Orlando, Florida—and ran right into his old buddy.

"We were both shocked," Davis said. "Neither of us could believe it for a minute." Holt was then an athlete at Western Kentucky University and on his way to a track meet. Davis was on his way to a photo session with the preseason Playboy All-America team.

They made small talk; Holt congratulated Davis, and then the friends said goodbye.

* * *

Whenever the Tigers needed a clutch play during their 9-3 Southeastern Conference championship season of 1986, Hodson, the precocious redshirt freshman quarterback, invariably went to Davis.

That, Hodson admitted looking back, surprised him as much as it surprised opposing secondaries.

Davis was not a hot catch in the recruiting class of 1984. LSU assistant Terry Lewis, who signed the 6-foot, 186-pound prospect, said in retrospect, "He looked like a normal little guy." Lewis, however, saw athletic potential in Davis, who wasn't eye-catching but solid in football at Fair Park High, and hit .543 in baseball—second in Shreveport only to future major-league All-Star Albert Belle.

It took a while to develop his superior receiving skills, though. After he signed, Hodson and Davis started working out together. Hodson, an accomplished passer, couldn't quite believe that Davis, who couldn't run under Hodson's long throws, and couldn't hang on to his short ones either, was actually a major-college athlete. "I was not overly impressed," Hodson said diplomatically with a smile. "Nothing exceptional."

Davis did have a very strong work ethic, though. He practiced tirelessly and ran precise, disciplined routes. He worked on his hand-eye coordination, and eventually began to make routine catches regularly. "The patterns," he said, "came before the hands." Then difficult catches began sticking in Davis' hands. His speed in the 40-yard dash improved from 5.0 seconds to 4.6.

"My father is the person I thank for that," Davis said. The work ethic was instilled in Wendell throughout his adolescence. No matter what outside interests Wendell had, they were to be enjoyed only after family chores were completed.

"I had to do things around the house—cut the grass, empty the trash, you know, odd jobs," Davis recalled of his youth. "But I had to do them. Football and other things came after my duties at home. My parents taught me discipline."

Davis' father, a crew chief in a Shreveport water district, may have been responsible for some of the most precise pass routes ever run in the SEC. Wendell thought so.

When Jackie Sherrill, then the head coach at Texas A&M, met Davis at an NCAA track meet held at LSU in the spring of 1987, he thought on first impression that the self-made receiver was a veteran pro athlete. "I thought he was a 28-, 29-year-old pro player back for the

Wendell Davis left LSU with a raft of records.

weekend. He's an impressive person. I don't think anyone has stopped him."

No one did. When Hodson took over the No. 1 quarterback duties as a redshirt freshman, he had a ready-made, polished target to throw to: Davis.

Hodson passed for 2,261 yards and 19 touchdowns in 1986—the season his primary receiver, Davis, led the NCAA in total receptions and touchdown receptions. The pair was college football's equivalent of the Dynamic Duo as LSU again won the SEC. There was more of the same in 1987.

"Those first two seasons [with Davis] were storybook seasons," Hodson said. "We had really great personnel and won a lot of games."

Davis left the LSU as the SEC's most productive receiver (2,708 yards), and the No. 1 draft choice of the Chicago Bears.

* * *

A budding pro career came to a sudden halt in a 1993 game at Philadelphia when Davis made a leap for a high pass. He came down hard and off-balance, and the patella tendons in both knees were shredded.

After long rehabilitation, Davis hooked up briefly with the Indianapolis Colts, but he was no longer the athlete he once was and called it quits.

"It wasn't my plan, it was God's plan, and I accept that," Davis said. "In a way I'm glad it happened because the challenge of overcoming it made me a better person, and the challenge of finding my way in a whole new lifestyle has made me a better person."

Staying in Chicago, Davis went into business. He owns two hair styling and cutting outlets, "Major League Barbers," and is also involved in manufacturing ventures.

"I'm still a rabid Tiger fan," he said. "I make trips home for games every season. I was there for the [2005] Auburn game when [former LSU receiver] Michael Clayton went on the field at halftime to present a check for Hurricane Katrina victims. They read his receiving records over the loud speaker before the presentation.

"A friend I was with leaned over and asked, 'Don't you still own any records?'

"One, I think," Davis said.

* * *

LSU had the perfect antidote for South Carolina's constant blitzes. The Tigers often used eight blockers and only two receivers on passing plays. The result was zero sacks; and quarterback Tom Hodson, who was chased out of the pocket or threw the ball away under pressure less than five times in 32 attempts, was not intercepted. LSU gained 346 yards against the vaunted Black Death.

The resultant consequence of a blitz, of course, is forced one-on-one coverage in the secondary—which played to LSU's strength. "That's what any receiver dreams about," Davis said. "I think we made them pay. It was fun at the end, after all the talking they had done before the game, yelling at each other, 'That was your man,' 'No, you should have picked him up!' I enjoyed that."

McKernan, the Gamecock linebacker, said afterward: "You've got to give it to them. They planned well for us. They had an idea what we were going to do and their idea was right. The only question was whether they could handle [the blitz]," McKernan said. "We didn't think they could. Obviously, we were wrong."

That error in judgment made Davis the man who killed the Black Death.

CHAPTER 9

RONNIE ESTAY

LSU 28 - Notre Dame 8
November 20, 1971 • Tiger Stadium

If there's anything close to a sure thing in football, this is it: fourth down and an inch to go—with the ball just four inches from the end zone.

Notre Dame went for it. Halfback Andy Huff propelled himself aloft behind the big Irish offensive line into the teeth—some might say heart—of the LSU defense, and was shot down before he could make any headway.

"I had to get high," LSU lineman Ronnie Estay recalled of the play that set the tone for the rest of the evening. "We stacked up their line, and I hit the runner in the air."

To use a boxing cliché to describe what transpired that night, Notre Dame could run, but the Irish couldn't hide.

They tried the left side, the right side, and up the middle. They tried running at undersized but super-quick tackle Ronnie Estay, then they started running away from him. Everywhere they went, though, Estay kept stuffing backs almost as big as his own dimensions of 6-feet-1, 230 pounds.

In a game in which many Tigers stood tall, one in which Notre Dame won the battle of statistics but handily lost the war of the scoreboard, this was the most important stat: seven times on fourth down the Irish went for the yardage. The three times Notre Dame did so inside the Tiger 10—once the aforementioned foot from the LSU goal, once inside the LSU 10, and once at the LSU 3—the Irish came up short.

The prime reason was Estay, a fiery Cajun playing the game of his collegiate life.

In the first instance, trailing 7-0 in the first quarter, Notre Dame got a gift in the form of a fumble recovery at the LSU 17. The Irish, behind an offensive line that averaged 250 pounds and dwarfed the Tiger defenders, wormed their way to the 1. The crowd was howling, almost as one, as Estay, then a swarm of Tigers, engulfed Huff.

That was a foreshadowing of what was to come on a night that Estay had 17 tackles—13 solo with four assists—in a football catharsis in which LSU eased the frustrations of two long years against the Irish.

* * *

Of course, Notre Dame, the premier football-playing university in the sporting world, has a target on its jersey each and every time its team suits up. Everyone loves to beat the Irish.

This, though, wasn't just a game for LSU fans—it was a crusade.

Two years before, with an offense that averaged 35 points a game and the best defense in the country, one that yielded just 389 rushing *all season*, LSU got caught up in bowl politics. The Tigers were unofficially ticketed to go to the Cotton Bowl to play No. 1 Texas—a team the LSU staff felt was tailor-made for them—and perhaps sneak off with the national championship. Shortly thereafter, the Irish secretly decided to break their long-time bowl ban and take the shot at the Longhorns themselves.

It was a chance no bowl could pass up. Except no one informed LSU. "I don't think shocked is a strong enough word," then-Tiger assistant Dave McCarty said of the reaction when LSU found out—after

Ronnie Estay (78) nails Auburn's Pat Sullivan for a safety.

Coach Charlie McClendon called Dallas to inquire why the Cotton representatives hadn't given him a ring—that it had been jilted.

By that time all the major bowls had been filled. The crushed Tigers could have accepted a smaller bowl bid, but voted as a team not to go anywhere.

It was really a matter of timing and circumstance—and of the Cotton Bowl not keeping LSU informed of the changing situation—but many inflamed Tiger fans blamed Notre Dame.

In 1970, the Tigers fielded a spectacular defense—again the nation's best against the run—one that had its chance against No. 1-ranked Notre Dame in South Bend.

In a glorious defensive spectacle, two-touchdown underdog LSU held Notre Dame, which had been rushing to the tune of 304 yards a game, to a ground total of 78. After an LSU field goal was blocked, then after a controversial interference call against the Tigers, the Irish kicked a 24-yard field goal with 2:54 to play and won 3-0.

The game was an epic, causing *Chicago Tribune* sportswriter Dave Condon to say in print the next morning, "If Notre Dame is No. 1, then LSU is No. 1-A."

That fueled a year-long obsession with the Irish among LSU fans. For the first time in memory, longtime SEC rivals Alabama and Ole Miss were mere afterthoughts when talk turned to football in the spring and summer. The clamor for tickets started in early spring, and when they went on sale every ticket was gone in a matter of hours—despite the fact that the game was scheduled for national television.

Temperatures went even higher when Irish coach Ara Parseghian said before the season that his team was physically the best he'd seen during his tenure at Notre Dame.

The Fightin' Tigers were 6-3 entering the game, and Notre Dame was ranked seventh with an 8-1 record, losing only to Southern Cal. Still, LSU was a one-point favorite.

The fervor in Baton Rouge before kickoff seemed even more intense than the Tiger-Ole Miss games of the late '50s and early '60s.

"We really wanted them," Estay said. "We felt like they were responsible for some bad breaks for LSU, and to be truthful we wanted some kind of revenge."

* * *

To an outsider looking in, Estay would be the stereotypical Louisianian. Growing up along Bayou Lafourche, dotted with settlements of Cajuns—descendents of the French-speaking Acadians of Nova Scotia who were driven from Canada by the British to escape a kind of 18th Century "ethnic cleansing"—Estay had an idyllic youth. He often ran barefoot, fished with a cane pole, rabbit hunted, and played football, all in the heart of what Cajuns enjoy calling "coonass country," where the zesty people speak with a fractured dialect of French and English.

The biggest problem he ever had with college football, he said, was having to speak strictly English. "Back home," he said at LSU, "all we talk is French. [Tailback] Art Cantrelle [from a neighboring town] is the only other fellow on the team I can talk French to."

There was never a problem on the field, though. Estay holds a distinction that would be difficult for anyone to equal. In the Tigers' 1970 SEC championship season, he nailed two Heisman Trophy contenders—Auburn's Pat Sullivan and Ole Miss' Archie Manning—for safeties. "He is the finest defensive tackle we've had at LSU since Fred Miller [a 1962 All-American]," McClendon said in the summer of '71. "There is no end to his endurance. It always seems corny to talk about 'love of the game.' But no player I've ever coached found more enjoyment playing football than Ronnie Estay."

There was one other, Ronnie would insist—his older brother, Maxie, who was a promising redshirt defensive lineman preparing for his first varsity season at LSU in 1965 when he was killed in an auto accident.

Ronnie picked up the torch.

At the wake, Ronnie said, "I told Coach McClendon that I'd be at LSU someday playing for him."

* * *

The Irish couldn't hide from LSU's fiery Cajun, Ronnie Estay.

Six years later Estay was lining up for what he still regards as the biggest game of his career, an LSU showcase that shot Estay onto the postseason All-America squads.

What sports fans witnessed that night on national television was an awesome—and unforgettable—display of Tiger football.

Throwing a curve at Notre Dame, McClendon started second-string quarterback Bert Jones for the first time since a three-interception game against Colorado in the season opener. McClendon made his decision after the coin flip, and said later he was playing a hunch, not only that the strong-armed backup could do serious damage to the Irish secondary but that Jones, at 6-feet-3, would be able to see over the huge Notre Dame line better than the Lyons, who was 5-feet-10.

In less than three minutes, Jones drove the Bayou Bengals 77 yards to a 7-0 lead as he hit his cousin, Andy Hamilton, on a 36-yard touchdown strike.

A possession later came a Jones fumble and, eventually, Notre Dame's failed attempt from inside the 1.

It didn't end there, although by this time the Irish seemed to be making a concerted effort to stay clear of Estay's side. That eliminated one side of the field for the Irish, meaning Estay was contributing even when he wasn't in on some tackles.

Notre Dame threatened again with a third-and-two feet at the LSU 10. The runner was stopped for no gain. Ara Parseghian couldn't believe what he was seeing and again passed up a field-goal attempt to go for it on fourth down. LSU should have made a believer out of him at that point because defensive back Norm Hodgins eluded a blocker as he fired into the backfield and nailed quarterback Cliff Brown for a three-yard loss.

Notre Dame's frustration put the crowd in a near-feeding frenzy. People sitting side by side could barely hear each other through the din.

For a third time in the first half, Notre Dame came charging back to the LSU 3, where, on fourth down, the Irish again decided to try for the touchdown. This time, though, Brown went to the air. He rolled to his right and lofted a pass intended for Larry Parker in the end zone. Cornerback Barton Frye seemingly came out of nowhere, reached calmly over Parker's shoulder, and batted the ball away.

After sophomore linebacker Warren Capone intercepted Brown, LSU finally had some breathing room.

The Tigers made the most of it. With 1:14 remaining in the first half, Jones again hit Hamilton for 32 yards and a 14-0 lead.

The game was essentially over, the Tigers inflicting what was then the worst defeat of Parseghian's Notre Dame career.

"Yes," the Irish coach said in hindsight, "we did consider field-goal attempts, but the distances were so short that they were worth the gambles—and we didn't make it."

Notre Dame led statistically in almost all categories. The Irish had 18 first downs to LSU's 14; had 323 totals yards to LSU's 299; and ran 84 plays to LSU's 60.

And yet LSU was way, way ahead in big, game-changing plays. The heroes were everywhere: Jones completed seven-of-nine passes for 143 yards and figured in three Tiger touchdowns; Hamilton caught seven passes for 153 yards and three touchdowns; Capone finished with two interceptions.

No statistic, though, stood out like Estay's 17 tackles.

"To this day," said Estay, who went on to a Hall of Fame playing career in the Canadian Football League, "sometimes I think of that game. I played in nine Grey Cups, and I may never have had more fun playing football than I did that night against Notre Dame."

Perhaps as satisfying as anything is the fact that the defeat nettled the Irish almost as much as their victory did LSU the year before.

Greg Marx, the Irish's 6-foot-5, 235-pound defensive tackle, reflected Notre Dame's frustration.

As LSU was attempting its fourth PAT in the final quarter, Marx gave Tiger guard Lloyd Daniels a shot to the leg. As the two got up, in a voice dripping with sarcasm and frustration, Marx said to Daniels, "Well, how do you like that, you [censored]?"

Daniels got up, pointed to the scoreboard, and answered, "Okay—how do you like that?"

CHAPTER 10

KEVIN FAULK

LSU 35 - Houston 34
September 7, 1996 • Tiger Stadium

"Bring Back the Magic," was Gerry DiNardo's coaching mantra at LSU. In his second season, after four years of football misery under Curley Hallman, Tiger Stadium's old bewitching persona was supposed to be restored.

Winning was back, bowls were back. In one year, DiNardo had folks believing in LSU again.

Then his second season opened, and, if anything, this was Black Magic—voodoo. The Tigers seemed hexed.

"Everything we did early seemed to backfire," Kevin Faulk, then a sophomore tailback, understated. "We were playing against ourselves as much as Houston."

Indeed. LSU, a 23-point favorite over Houston, already 1-0 on the season, turned the ball over five times, miscues that led to 24 Cougar points and put the 17th-ranked Tigers in jeopardy of losing the opening game of what was anticipated to be a big season.

Going into the fourth quarter, with some disgruntled fans scurrying for the exits and other staying but venting their displeasure with boos, the Tigers were shockingly behind by 20 points. How frustrating an evening was it? At the end of three quarters, LSU was ahead of Houston on the stat sheet, 400 yards to 228, and behind on the scoreboard 34-14.

All LSU had going for it at this point was No. 3, Faulk, who actually contributed as much as anyone to the hole from which LSU had to dig itself. Already having an outstanding game statistically, Faulk was the catalyst of a remarkable Tiger comeback. Before all was said and done, he fired the LSU offense to 601 yards. Faulk carried 21 times for a school-record 246 yards, returned four punts for another 106 yards, had 16 yards in kickoff returns, and caught a pass for eight yards. It all added up to 376 all-purpose yards, best in Tiger annals.

"If you want to call it a great game, okay, but I fumbled two times," Faulk said immediately afterward, referring to two loose balls the Cougars converted into 14 points.

Fair enough, but few doubt that, without him, the Tigers wouldn't have roared back—not just from the precipice of defeat but from humiliation against a program with just three victories in the previous four seasons. On the first play of the final quarter, Faulk took a Houston punt, gave a juke, got some running space, and outran the Cougar coverage 78 yards to the end zone.

"We had a big discussion on the sidelines about whether to kick to Kevin or not," Cougar back (and later a pro teammate) Antwain Smith said. Faulk, now a member of the New England Patriots, said, "I guess they decided to take the chance."

No, they didn't. The Houston brain trust decided to kick away from Faulk. But the punt went right to him. "Coach really chewed our punter out when he got back to the sidelines," Smith remembered.

Houston paid the price for the kick—and more than just the touchdown. That miscalculation ignited a Tiger rampage resulting in LSU outscoring the visitors 21-0 and out-gaining them 201 yards to 49 in the final 15 minutes. That surge allowed the Tigers to overcome the turnovers, which resulted in 130 yards for the Cougars on interception and fumble returns.

If ever there was one, this seemed like a job for Superman—Faulk's childhood hero and whose symbol of a triangle with the letter "S" in the middle is tattooed on his left bicep.

* * *

The thing Faulk most clearly remembers of the 1996 opener was that he didn't know if he would play. "I was suspended," he said.

Involved in an off-season altercation outside a bar in his hometown of Carencro, Louisiana, Faulk was charged with four misdemeanor counts, including two counts of battery on a police officer. DiNardo dropped him from the squad, pending its resolution.

"The thing about it was, I wasn't even part of the fight," Faulk said. "I was trying to stop it and was caught up in the confusion."

Just before the Houston game, the charges were dropped and Faulk was reinstated, irritating Houston's coach, Kim Helton, who knew he could be the difference.

DiNardo knew it, too, and hitched his early LSU coaching star to the elusive and uncommonly strong 5-foot-10, 195-pound back. A six-year drought in which LSU went 28-45 under Mike Archer and Hallman—16-28 under the latter—during which the Tigers endured their worst season (2-9 in 1992) and worst defeat (58-3 to Florida in 1993), brought DiNardo to LSU. On the day he got the job, he made the 50-mile trip from Baton Rouge to Carencro to visit the No. 1 prospect in the state. Faulk, an option quarterback in high school whose future was clearly as a runner on the next level, had staggering statistics: 4,877 rushing yards, 89 touchdowns, and 7,612 yards of total offense.

The new coach knew this kid could help bring back the magic. He also knew he had to beat out some heavyweight competition: Florida, Florida State, and Notre Dame were all in the running. What he didn't know was one of his main talking points was that 50-mile trip between Baton Rouge and Carencro. "When I took my visit to Notre Dame, my mom and dad went with me, and I still missed home," Faulk said. "I'm not ashamed to admit it, I'm a mama's boy."

Along with the birth of Faulk's daughter, that proximity was the eventual tiebreaker between the Gators and the Tigers.

Kevin Faulk started the fireworks against Houston.

Sure enough, the next year LSU was again competitive, taking toddling steps back to respectability with a 7-4-1 record, including an Independence Bowl victory over Nick Saban's Michigan State Spartans. Faulk was the Tigers' leading 1995 rusher, gaining 852 yards and was the SEC Freshman Offensive Player of the Year.

The fact that Faulk might not play in the 1996 season opener must have emboldened Helton, who commented days before the game that Tiger Stadium was just another place where football is played, incensing the LSU faithful.

The Houston coach was equally infuriated when, two days before the game, Faulk was reinstated.

* * *

For a while, it looked as if the whole LSU team was either suspended or playing in a state of suspended animation.

The crowd of 80,303 spectators couldn't wait to give Helton a dose of Tiger Stadium vituperation for his blasphemy. But they were silenced. Not so much by Houston but by their own stumbling Tigers—including Faulk. Just before the half, he fumbled to set up a Cougar touchdown which gave Houston a 20-7 lead with 22 seconds remaining.

He redeemed himself on the first play of the third quarter when, on a counter-play, Faulk shot past the line and wheeled into the startled secondary, going 80 yards for the touchdown. "When I realized I was in the open I started thinking, 'Don't let anyone catch you now.' When I hit the end zone I was relieved," Faulk recalled.

The relief was short-lived. LSU started moving again, but Tiger tight end David LaFleur, running for a first down, dropped the ball on the Houston 12. It was picked up by a Cougar and returned 61 yards, setting up the Houston touchdown that made the score 27-14 when the PAT was missed. Just minutes later, Faulk—squirming for extra yardage on a 10-yard sweep—fumbled again with Stedman Forman picking it up and running it back 30 yards to give Houston its 20-point lead.

Five minutes and 57 seconds later, the fireworks would be ignited.

Faulk ran back the punt to cut the margin to 34-21, and LSU put together another drive to make the score 34-28, then another to almost unbelievably go up 35-34.

Faulk muffed yet another ball, this time on a punt. Yet, perhaps a sign the Tigers' luck had turned, he managed to recover the loose ball. During LSU's final possession—on third-and-one—Faulk, with his trademark burst of speed, motored 43 yards. Those two plays may have saved the signature performance of Faulk's notable career.

By the time the '96 season was over, Faulk had amassed 1,282 yards rushing with 13 touchdowns, and another 822 yards in pass receptions and kick returns. When he was placed on the Associated Press' All-America first team as a sophomore, it was as an all-purpose player. It was fitting because Faulk finished his college career fifth on the all-time NCAA list for all-purpose yardage (6,833) and second only to Georgia's Herschel Walker in the SEC in rushing yardage (4,553) and rushing touchdowns (46).

"He's a thing of grace and beauty," teammate Herb Tyler said admiringly of Faulk, who led the Tigers in rushing each of his four years at LSU.

Looking back, Houston turned out to be a magic moment. No one can remember the Tigers coming back from so far in the last 15 minutes, but unquestionably this was LSU's biggest comeback since rallying from a 21-0 halftime deficit against Ole Miss in 1977. It was also one of the rare times anyone ever came back from so deep a hole without aerial support. After falling behind by 20, the Tigers passed only five times—and LSU rolled up its massive yardage yards against what turned out to be a pretty decent team. Houston went on to win the first Conference USA championship.

"It turned out to be a positive for us," said Antwain Smith. "Losing by one point at LSU kind of showed us we could play with anybody."

LSU, too, straightened out, tying for first place in the SEC West and completing a 10-2 season in the Peach Bowl.

* * *

Kevin Faulk showed the Cougars his all-purpose wares.

Kim Helton was steaming in the Houston locker room. "I think the greatest thing that happened to them was the fact that their coach changed his mind and let No. 3 play," he said later, ignoring the fact that there was no longer a reason for Faulk to be punished. "No. 3 got unsuspended and made a lot of runs," Helton assessed. "He's a talented guy."

In the aftermath, Helton had to second-guess himself. Because of his decisions the door was cracked just wide enough for the Tigers. When Houston went ahead 27-14, Helton went for a one-point PAT instead of trying to make the score in multiples of seven (28-14). The Cougars kicked again when the score mounted to 34-14.

"We missed a two-point conversion earlier," he explained, "and we missed one last week. So we went for one. At that point, I didn't think they'd get back in the game."

Faulk remembered the game from a different vantage point. "It was frustrating," he recalled, "because we kept stopping ourselves. We were happy to win but pretty mad at ourselves afterward."

Faulk went on to play on three Super Bowl championship teams in New England, where he's used as a third-down back.

"We're a team where everyone has a role," Faulk said. "When we all do what we're supposed to do we have success—a lot of success. I've been blessed."

CHAPTER 11

MAX
FUGLER

LSU 14 - Ole Miss 0
November 1, 1958 • Tiger Stadium

As the down marker flipped over to show the numeral "2," Max Fugler thought to himself, "That is a *big* mistake."

It was. After all, Ole Miss had given up an extra snap to keep the ball where it was. And the Rebels still had to traverse the rest of the way to the end zone—a foot, 12 full inches.

The sixth-ranked Rebels, as good a program as there was in America at the time, were poised to land a body-blow to the Tigers, newly—and precariously—perched at the top of the college football world. Leaning over the ball during the snap count, the Ole Miss helmets already seemed halfway over the plane of the end zone. Fugler, playing linebacker, looking back, exclaimed, "That's just how close they were."

And how close the Tigers came to absorbing what could have been a fatal shot to what became the most fabled season in Tiger annals, the undefeated, untied, national championship of 1958.

Here, at the start of the second quarter, at the fringe of the south end zone, was the seminal moment in modern LSU football. Everything we now associate with the Tigers—decades of title-contending teams, a litany of All-Americans making breathtaking plays, a regularly filled-beyond-capacity stadium—flowed from what happened at this point.

Alter the sequence, and LSU might have lost and not have been No. 1 at season's end; all the area athletes, who at the time were attracted to the colorful and exciting Tiger program, might have gone elsewhere.

Although the game against Kentucky two weeks earlier filled the seats, this game was the first hard sellout since Tiger Stadium was expanded by 19,000 seats to 67,510 in 1954.

The Ole Miss game, though, brought a new football phenomenon to Baton Rouge: ticket scalping. There was more demand than seats. Tiger Stadium is routinely sold out now with LSU's tens of thousands of season-ticket holders. But who knows, a disappointing setback here, and fan interest could have again shrunk to the level of 9,000 season-ticket holders LSU had just a year earlier, a level befitting a program with just four winning seasons in the previous 10.

To comprehend how much could have changed with the outcome of this game is almost inconceivable.

But it didn't.

Ole Miss halfback Kent Lovelace set the scene when he barreled down to the LSU 2-yard line, giving the Rebels a first and goal. Quarterback Bobby Franklin tried to wedge his way in behind Ole Miss' large line, and got within a foot of a touchdown.

Here's where the legend grows.

The Tigers were offside. The Rebels could have a first-and-goal at the 1, or decline the penalty and take a second-and-a foot. Could any team hold Ole Miss, with three shots, from making mere inches? The Rebels didn't think so, and took the play.

This is the ensuing sequence:

- On second-and-a foot, Lovelace went off-tackle. End Red Hendrix, tackle Lynn LeBlanc, and Fugler stuffed him for no gain;
- On third-and-a foot, fullback Charlie Flowers tried the middle and was dropped just short of the line of scrimmage by Fugler;
- On fourth-and-a foot, the Rebels bypassed a field-goal attempt, and with Tiger Stadium a cauldron of sound and emotional fury for both sides, Lovelace again tried to go off-tackle, and was swarmed by the Tiger defense, including Billy Cannon's glancing blow before Fugler—who was in on every tackle of this remarkable stand— dropped him for a yard loss.

Max Fugler was an immovable object in a monumental LSU stand.

Fugler felt a measure of satisfaction as he watched the down marker flipped again, to "1" and forcefully threw out his arm indicating it was LSU's ball and the direction the Tigers were moving. His instinct about Ole Miss foregoing the penalty that started the goal-line series was proved correct.

"They never did figure our scheme out," Fugler said. "They apparently thought we were in a five-man front, and we kept slipping into a seven. [Defensive assistant] Charlie McClendon kept yelling to me not to change what we were doing, and they never did pick me up.

"After that, with the tremendous emotional charge it gave us, we didn't think anybody or anything could stop us."

This is how you know luck is running your way: Later in the second quarter, Rebel back Billy Brewer fumbled on the Ole Miss 21, and LSU recovered. On fourth-and-goal from the 4, with 25 seconds remaining until the half, quarterback Warren Rabb took a snap from Fugler and rolled out. His receivers covered, Rabb cut toward the end zone and was hit at the 2. As he was going down, another Rebel slammed into the falling bodies, propelling Rabb across the goal.

Such are the ways in which national championships are won.

With a touchdown lead and his players performing at a fever pitch, Coach Paul Dietzel, usually as buttoned-down as a vest, told his team, "You beat Ole Miss when you stopped them at the goal line!"

LSU went on to a fourth-quarter touchdown and a 14-0 victory, marking the first time the heralded Ole Miss offense had been shut out in 15 games.

It was an eye-catching performance, earning Fugler national lineman of the week recognition. Remembering it at season's end apparently didn't hurt either as he made All-America.

More than that, the game became a college football classic, with memories that reverberate still on both sides. "I've thought about that game many times in the years since we played it," said Billy Brewer, who a quarter-century later was the Rebels' head coach. "I really believe that was the start of big-time football in the South. I'm proud we were a part of it. The spirit of those people in that stadium, then and now, is unmatched anywhere. It was a game to remember."

Dietzel placed the postgame laurels squarely on the defense in general and Fugler in particular. "One time," he marveled, "Fugler tackled the quarterback and made him pitch. Then he got off the ground and tackled the ball carrier. He actually made two tackles on the same play."

* * *

Obviously, the times made Louisiana a football wonderland—and especially for Fugler, who matriculated to LSU from a famed team in Ferriday that won 54 straight games. Fugler's teams went 38-1 and won three state championships.

"Heck," he said, "I don't recall losing a game until I was a sophomore in college." His combined high school and college record is 68-8-0. "Not bad, huh?" Fugler, a junior in '58, said devilishly.

Not bad at all—but, looking back, he was lucky to be with the starting unit against Ole Miss.

It was a time when the substitution rules dictated that players played both ways, and the athlete who was by far the best center/linebacker at LSU was not Fugler. Another player named Doug Skinner, part of the incoming freshman class of 1956 with Billy Cannon, Johnny Robinson and Fugler, was. "He was the roughest, toughest Tiger of them all," said Joe May, a former LSU halfback and assistant coach who has observed every LSU team up close since 1953. "Man, that guy took no prisoners, at practice or in games. I felt bad for everyone who had to play against Doug."

Skinner was so impressive that in the 1957 season he forced one of Dietzel's prized recruits, Fugler, to change positions from the line to the backfield. "And, heck, he deserved it," Fugler said matter-of-factly.

About midseason, though, Skinner disappeared.

"Everyone said me and Billy [Cannon] would be All-Americans," Skinner, retired in Texas, said 40 years later. "You don't always take advantage of the opportunities that come your way, and I sure didn't. I had a few problems, and they left me behind on a road trip. There wasn't anything to do in Baton Rouge, so I went home."

And never returned.

Fugler went back to his old position. The rest is history.

* * *

If Rebel coach Johnny Vaught had his way, Fugler would have been donned in Ole Miss red and blue for that game.

A highly recruited kid—what we'd call now call a national recruit—Fugler said tongue-in-cheek he wasn't sure he could take the big-city life of Oxford, Mississippi. His choices came down to Southern Cal, Michigan State, and LSU, which Fugler chose mainly for the twin reasons of proximity and its respected petroleum-engineering school.

Fugler apparently made the right choice in the classroom and on the field, as LSU ran through a series of coaching legends-in-the-making during the '58 season: The Tigers opened on the road against defending Southwest Conference champion Rice, and Jess Neely, a Hall of Fame coach. LSU won 26-6.

Alabama, playing its first game under Bear Bryant, was LSU's second opponent, and the Tigers won 13-3.

Hardin-Simmons, a pass-happy breather coached by the fabled old TCU and Redskins quarterback Sammy Baugh, was LSU's home opener, attended by 45,000 fans—LSU won 20-6.

Miami, coached by the respected Andy Gustafson, represented the Tigers' fourth victory, 41-0.

Kentucky, coached by Blanton Collier—one of the finest tacticians in football history—was then beaten 32-7.

Venerable Bob Woodruff was the coach of the Florida Gators who LSU beat in the fading seconds, 10-7.

That Vaught would have a place in that string of LSU opponents was fitting because Ole Miss represented a clear measure of how far the Tigers had come. Dietzel thought Vaught hung the moon, and said, "We learned a lot from John Vaught. He was a fine fellow and a great coach."

Ole Miss administered a painful lesson on the value of quality depth. The Tigers led the Rebels 17-14 at the half of their 1956 game. "We played as well as we could play," Dietzel said. "But by the time we got to the dressing room, we were worn out. "The Rebels routed LSU in the second half, chalking up a 46-17 victory.

After that game, Dietzel started tinkering with substitution plans that, two years later, were his acclaimed three-team system—with a platoon of quality two-way players (the White Team), another of offensive specialists (The Go Team), and a third of defensive specialists (The Chinese Bandits).

That, of course, played a role in the outcome of their game in 1958—along with Fugler on the goal line, a prospect that got away from Vaught.

* * *

Between his junior and senior seasons, Fugler, a petroleum engineering major, took a summer job with a Houston oil company named Hycalog, owned by LSU graduates J.R. Mayeaux and Dan Grady. That set the tone for his professional career.

Drafted by the San Francisco 49ers after the '59 season, Fugler tore up his knee in the seventh game of his rookie season. He never played football again.

His old bosses offered Fugler a full-time opportunity, which he accepted and stayed in for 11 years.

Then Fugler formed his own oil-service company, Gammaloy, Inc., which he operated for 31 years before selling it to Tom Hicks, owner of the Texas Rangers and Dallas Stars. He still works for Gammaloy under the new management.

No one, though, Fugler said, asks him about his business acumen as often they inquire about his performance that memorable night against Ole Miss.

He agrees that goal-line stand was the centerpiece moment in the centerpiece game of the '58 season, but added:

"It was more than that," Fugler said. "It was the centerpiece of my career."

CHAPTER 12

DEVERY HENDERSON

LSU 33 - Kentucky 30
November 9, 2002 • Lexington, Kentucky

It took a while to sink in. Minutes—even hours—later fans of both LSU and Kentucky were shaking their heads in disbelief.

How much disbelief? Well, Kentucky students were already flooding one side of the of the field before the clock expired, readying for an assault on the goal posts; the coach was already soaked from a Gatorade bath; a fireworks display to celebrate a Wildcat victory over the Bayou Bengals was already lighting up the skies over Commonwealth Stadium.

Jefferson-Pilot, televising the game, had already flashed the score as a final: Kentucky 30, LSU 27.

Oops.

"It was like you weren't watching what happened," Jimbo Fisher, the LSU offensive coordinator who called the play from the pressbox, was babbling in disbelief immediately afterward. "You were numb. It was just a freak, unbelievable thing."

That it was. Here's the scenario. On the last play of the game, with two seconds remaining, LSU was three points down and 75 yards away from the end zone.

Breaking loose after a reception is dangerous Devery Henderson.

Devery Henderson entered Tiger folklore by being, more or less, in the right place at the right time on a classic "last-play" call—one that never once worked in months of LSU practices. The play—Dash-right-93 Berlin—was basically a "Hail Mary," a throw-the-ball-and-pray-type play.

Prayers are sometimes answered, and this one was.

The pigskin missile launched by quarterback Marcus Randall, who let loose with all the arm strength he had, was in the air for 68 yards. When the ball finally came down in the blur of blue, white, and gold colors, safety Quentus Cumby got a finger on it before it slipped through the fingers of linebacker Morris Lane, then cornerback Earven Flowers tipped it. Henderson took it out of the air at the 18, juggling the ball for three yards before running through a tackle attempt by cornerback Derrick Tatum and on into the end zone. There, Henderson euphorically threw his arms to the skies, making himself almost a human version of the "V for victory" sign.

About that instant is when Jefferson-Pilot made the correction: LSU 33, Kentucky 30.

"We practice that play every week," the quiet and humble Henderson said. "But it never works. [Receiver] Michael [Clayton] was supposed to be the tip man, but the tip guys turned out to be Kentucky players. How can you figure something like that? All I remember was bobbling the ball, then pulling it in, then running like hell."

* * *

The stunning turn of events placed LSU in the select company of programs with jarring, unlikely last-gasp nationally-televised victories that fans everywhere can remember where and when they saw it, and will for decades to come: Doug Flutie's famed pass that lifted Boston College over Miami; Kordell Stewart's end-of-the-game pass for Colorado to beat Michigan; the unforgettable kickoff return by California against Stanford in which Cal players kept pitching the ball backward until the last man with the ball ran into the end zone—and into the Stanford tuba player in one of the most memorable moments of college football history.

The victory gave LSU—a good team but one rebuilding from the personnel losses from 2001—a 7-2 record and the illusion it could defend its SEC championship. The Tigers, however, knew full well they were every bit as lucky against Kentucky, 6-3 entering the game, as they were good—a condition confirmed by LSU linebacker coach Kirk Doll, who said in the locker room afterward, "The first thing I'm going to do when I get back to Baton Rouge is buy a lottery ticket."

* * *

Despite the presence of All-America receiver Michael Clayton, and despite the fact that Henderson was not a natural pass-catcher, spending his first two seasons at LSU as a backup tailback, he had to be accounted for by opposing defensive coordinators. A 6-foot, 190-pound high-octane flyer, Henderson ran 4.41 in the 40-yard dash.

"Devery is extremely fast," LSU quarterback Matt Mauck said in an evaluation of his teammate at the time. "He came to LSU not as a receiver but as a running back. He's worked extremely hard at route-running. Since Devery's so fast, he always gives you something down field."

He did. However, originally Henderson, who has gone on to an NFL career with the New Orleans Saints, was thought to have the potential to be a game-breaker, but out of the backfield. At Opelousas (Louisiana) High, Henderson ran for more 2,800 yards and 33 touchdowns in his last two seasons. According to him, though, he only caught "two or three passes" in high school. In his first couple of years at LSU, Henderson carried the ball 70 times for fewer than 400 yards, and caught just one pass. Tiger coaches didn't really know what to do with him.

"I was moving all around my first couple of years," he recalled. "Running back, defensive back, I was even at receiver briefly one time before. Coach Saban said that with the talent I have, I should be playing somewhere."

Eventually, the permanent move to receiver was made, and as a junior he caught 23 passes for 447 yards and eight TDs before breaking his arm against Ole Miss.

"Everything was tough for me that first year as a receiver," Henderson recalled later. "A lot of times I got frustrated. Catching the ball was not tough, but I had to learn little things, like going the right depth on routes."

He did get the knack, becoming one of the most dangerous deep-receiving threats in college football. After switching to receiver permanently, Henderson caught 74 passes for 1,284 yards, and one rather eye-popping statistic: More than one-fourth (19) of those receptions produced touchdowns.

As a senior, when LSU won the BCS national championship, Henderson caught 51 passes for 837 yards and 11 touchdowns—second in school annals to teammate Clayton's 21 for most scoring receptions in a season.

Much of those in 2003 were done in dramatic fashion. Five of Henderson's touchdowns covered at least 46 yards. A 53-yard TD catch in the fourth quarter provided the winning points in LSU's 17-14 victory against Ole Miss; his 64-yard reception capped a scoring drive on the Tigers' first possession in their 31-7 victory against Auburn; he had touchdown catches of 56 yards against Arizona and 50 and 46 against Louisiana Tech.

"I'm just putting everything together now," he said at the time. "I just run my route and read the defense. Most of the time I come open."

Never was that more true than against Kentucky.

* * *

Somewhat lost in the retelling of "The Bluegrass Miracle" is the fact that Henderson didn't just come out of nowhere. He was a lightning rod that entire afternoon.

Early in the second quarter, with Kentucky ahead 7-0, Randall flipped a shovel pass to Henderson, who took it and shot 70 yards for the tying touchdown. Late in the period, Henderson caught two passes on a drive that ultimately covered 78 yards, the first for 23 yards, and the second for 30 yards for a go-ahead touchdown with five seconds remaining until halftime.

Henderson finished the day with five catches for 201 yards, a school record-tying 40.2 yards per reception, and three touchdowns.

Many things had to fall into line, though, for the theatrics to take place. The first was a coaching gaffe by Guy Morriss, who did not allow the clock to run completely down when he sent out Taylor Begley to kick a 29-yard field to break a 27-27 deadlock. Instead, after Begley's successful kick, there were 15 crucial seconds remaining.

Miracles can't be choreographed, but this one came close.

Henderson returned the ensuing kicking, intentionally running out of bounds at the LSU 13 with nine seconds left to save time. "Just the way he was coached," said Jimbo Fisher. After a delay-of-game penalty, Randall hit Clayton for 17 yards at the 25.

"He didn't even try to gain more yards," Fisher added.

"He just stepped out of bounds as soon as he made the catch with enough time for one play. It was a long shot, of course, but up to this point we played things perfectly."

The clock was stopped with those two precious seconds left.

Henderson, Clayton, and Reggie Robinson lined up to the right, and Jerel Myers to the left. Randall rolled right and waited for the receiving corp, all running pell mell, to get downfield. "In my head, I'm like, 'Let God be with us,'" Henderson recalled. "I ran down the field and just tried to put myself in position."

Nothing seemed to be going right. In this case, Dash-right-93 Berlin, which was designed for Robinson to make the tip to the sure-handed Clayton closest to the goal with Henderson moving on the quarterback side. Everyone was out of position, jostled by Kentucky defenders, and the ball sailed over the outstretched fingertips of Clayton—and into the cluster of mostly blue-shirted figures.

"It was like a dream," Henderson said. "I saw it tipped and tipped again. I reached out and it fell in my hands. I couldn't believe it. I just kept running, and all I saw were Kentucky fans, and I couldn't see the goal line. Then someone came and tackled me, then there was a pile on top of me."

The pile consisted of Henderson's victorious teammates.

The funny thing about it was, Henderson was more concerned with not being called out at film sessions as someone who didn't give the

Devery Henderson was the man of the hour against Kentucky.

necessary effort. "I didn't want that to happen," he said. What made it work, he said, was "… just more instinct and natural reaction than me thinking about what was going on."

But in the end, Henderson philosophized, "I guess it all goes to prove that football is a 60-minute game."

* * *

Another noted Tiger athlete was asked in Los Angeles days after the game about Henderson's heroics, and Shaquille O'Neal deadpanned, "At LSU, we're used to doing the impossible."

What goes around, though, comes around. In the season finale against Arkansas, with a second straight berth in the SEC championship game on the line, the Razorbacks traveled 77 yards in 25 seconds to beat LSU 21-20—the winning points coming on a 31-yard touchdown pass with nine seconds to play. Despite the fact that there was still time on the game clock, there would be no Ozark Miracle for LSU.

Still, the drama—and sheer inconceivability—of the Bluegrass Miracle caught everyone's fancy. It won an ESPY as the Play of the Year in all of sports in 2002, a ceremony that meant every bit as much to Henderson as the play that made it possible.

"It was special," Henderson said of his trip to Hollywood for the awards ceremony with his mother. "I got the opportunity to give my mom a trip out of Louisiana—Opelousas, specifically. She hadn't really been to too many places or had the chance to travel, and she had a good time. She even came on stage with me. I didn't bring her on stage. She just walked up. I want everyone to know, I was up there and looked back, and there she was."

CHAPTER 13

DALTON HILLIARD

LSU 55 - Florida State 21
November 20, 1982 • Tiger Stadium

The fog rolling in from the nearby Mississippi River—or the rainstorm of oranges flying down from the upper reaches of Tiger Stadium—might have been easier to stop. Dalton Hilliard spent the night gliding through, around, and over the defensive line of the Florida State Seminoles. The 5-foot-8, 185-pound freshman whirling dervish, amassed 183 yards rushing with three touchdowns plus another 50 yards and yet another touchdown receiving in a game in which 12th-ranked LSU simply demolished the seventh-ranked 'Noles for the right to go to the Orange Bowl—a victory in which rambunctious Tiger fans unleashed a shower of citrus that filled the filmy night sky.

"It just rained oranges," Hilliard recalled with a laugh. After a noteworthy career with the New Orleans Saints from which he retired as the club's all-purpose yardage leader, Hilliard opened and operates a contracting-services company for shipyard businesses in south Louisiana and Texas. Still an avid LSU fan, he said: "When people speak of the mystique of Tiger Stadium, I always think of that night with the oranges and the fog."

Dalton Hilliard was LSU's Little Big Man, and a major difference-maker.

That night of oranges and fog, a shell-shocked Bobby Bowden sat in the cramped locker room looking down and mumbling over and over, "Hillary beat us. We just couldn't stop Hillary."

When Bowden, given to malaprops, was eventually corrected and told the name of the white-shirted spirit wearing No. 21 that bedeviled his defense all night was "Hilliard," the roly-poly ringmaster of Florida State football smiled and said, "I still like the name 'Hillary.'"

No matter. LSU, now 8-1-1, was headed to Miami. Florida State (8-2) was shuttled to Jacksonville for the Gator Bowl.

The victory was especially sweet for LSU for a couple of reasons: the Tigers had lost three straight to the Seminoles; also there was a strain between the schools because ABC wanted to televise the game, but at what was then its prime football time, in the afternoon. LSU coach Jerry Stovall wanted to—and did—play in the Tigers' traditional nighttime setting.

"On this day," Bowden said, "LSU was better than any team we've played this season. They would have beat us at three o'clock in the morning, 12:30 in the afternoon, or four o'clock in the afternoon."

The main cause of that dissection was Hilliard, whose four touchdowns gave him 16 for the season—one more than the NCAA freshman record previously held by Georgia's Herschel Walker—and who Florida State simply couldn't contain.

One account said, "Hilliard scampered right, left, up the middle, squirming, it appeared, through keyholes, planting a foot, changing directions, faking a talented collection of athletes out of their athletic supporters."

It wasn't hyperbole.

LSU's first score came in the first quarter when Hilliard caught a pass, spun, then darted, almost going down twice before finding his way past two defenders and twinkle-toeing his way 46 yards to the end zone; he got another touchdown from the 2 with 39 seconds left until the half after carrying eight times in an 11-play drive, gaining 46 of 50 yards; LSU later went on 16-play drive that consumed the first 8:44 of the second half as Hilliard carried the ball 14 times, gaining 70 of the necessary 80 yards; and in the fourth quarter, he sprinted 28 yards and broke three tackles for his last touchdown.

His pronunciation now adjusted, Bowden said: "Hilliard was the difference."

* * *

Four months before, no one could believe—or would believe—the preseason depth chart at tailback. It read: Dalton Hilliard, Garry James, Gene Lang, Karl Bernard.

Dalton who? This had to be a psychological ploy by Coach Jerry Stovall. The fans weren't the only ones perplexed. Before that chart was released, backfield coach Darrell Moody had to tell his boss, "We've got a problem. Our third-string back is better than anyone we have."

Moody was speaking of the little-known Hilliard, a back who seemed to glide into a hole and then change speed and direction as if he were defying the laws of physics. Still, at that point, only a few observers knew of Hilliard, who was in select company since every one of the players on that list would see time in the NFL, and since Hilliard was shorter than the average LSU student.

LSU had to beat out the rest of the college football world for fellow freshman James, 6 feet, 2 inches, 200 pounds. Only Tulane was in the running for Hilliard, who came out of the small, south Louisiana town of Patterson in St. Mary Parish.

Even some of the Tiger coaches questioned playing a man so small, until LSU linebackers coach Buddy Nix, who first spotted Hilliard, reminded them all, "An offensive line opens holes that are wide, not high."

Stovall, nobody's fool, told Moody to keep the chart in order of productivity and nothing else.

Hilliard turned out to be a dazzling, exciting runner. His uncommon strength and agility was funneled through thigh muscles that appeared, at first glance, to be the size of a young human adult waist, 23 inches.

With those wheels, Hilliard became the first freshman running back in modern LSU history to draw a starting assignment in a season-opening game. He gained 133 yards and scored three touchdowns in that game against Oregon State, and the job was Hilliard's from then on, although James also starred in a backfield known in LSU lore as the "Dalton-James Gang."

When he left college four years later, the Tiger record book showed Hilliard as the best running back statistically in LSU history—one of only two Tigers to rush for more than 4,000 yards. Two games after his debut, he gained 127 yards in a 24-13 upset of Florida that propelled Hilliard into national consciousness. There was more in those figures than most people realized.

Moody kept two game charts—one listing the yards a back gained, the other listing yardage gained after being hit or after the ball-carrier made a defender miss a tackle. Against the Gators, Moody said, Hilliard shouldn't have gotten more than half the net yardage for which he received credit. Of the 127 yards he picked up, 73 came after he had been hit or after making a defender miss a tackle.

"He runs with his eyes as well as his feet," Stovall said.

Indeed. Consider this, Hilliard was not only still LSU's all-time leading rusher in 1993, LSU's football centennial year, but was also the Tigers' No. 9 all-time receiver with 1,133 yards on 119 catches, and LSU's leading scorer with 302 points.

Surely that fulfilled the promise Nix first saw in Hilliard.

Nix, who recruited James Brooks for Auburn, practically lived in Patterson for two years. "When I saw Dalton in the spring of his [high school] junior year, I said to myself, 'Well, here's another one,'" Nix said of the quick-footed back wearing No. 21. "He's even wearing Brooks' number. I told Darrell, 'I've found another Brooks.'"

That's part of the reason Hilliard was such a devastating runner: seldom did a defender get a clean shot at the gliding ghost, but when they did, they hit legs as sturdy as pillars. His leg muscles protrude like that of a body-builder.

"People were wondering if Dalton was big enough to take the punishment," Nix said after Hilliard set the NCAA freshman touchdown record. "Hell, nobody's had a clean tackle on him yet."

When he was injured in high school, Jo Ann Landry, the assistant principal at Patterson, drove Hilliard to a Napoleonville physician. She recalled: "We'd gotten to the doctor's office, and the nurse put Dalton on

Dalton Hilliard ran with his eyes as well as his feet.

the examination table. All of a sudden the doctor yelled, 'Jo Ann! Come see!' I thought something was really wrong with Dalton."

The doctor asked Dalton to flex the thigh muscles in his healthy leg. When he did, bands of muscle ballooned under the skin and the physician's eyes widened. "He said he'd never seen muscles like that," Landry chuckled, "even in medical school."

* * *

Those muscles carried Hilliard to 5,326 all-purpose yards for LSU. There was more to come. Again silencing some naysayers, LSU's Little Big Man went on to an eight-year career in the NFL, finishing with more touchdowns (53) and more all-purpose yards (7,449) than anyone in the history of the New Orleans Saints. One eye-catching statistic is the 228 yards Hilliard accumulated in completing eight halfback passes—that went for five touchdowns.

Jim Dombrowski, a Saints teammate, made as good an attempt as anyone at analyzing Hilliard's skills. "Dalton did an exceptional job of setting up his blocks, and once he got in the open field, his natural talents took over. He wasn't the fastest guy around, but you give me a five-foot square, and I'll put Dalton in there against anybody. He'll bust out the other side, and the other guy will be on the ground. Dalton had power, he was shifty, and he was tough."

The modest and soft-spoken Hilliard just said, "I've never been a great one for statistics—all I wanted to do was my job."

CHAPTER 14

TOMMY HODSON

LSU 7 - Auburn 6
October 8, 1988 • Tiger Stadium

The ground actually trembled, and there is undeniable proof:

LSU's stirring comeback against one Auburn's best teams—in as courageous a performance as any Tiger team ever turned in—produced a reaction which literally equaled a force of nature.

Over the years, it has even acquired a title: "The Night the Tigers Shook the Earth" is how it will forevermore be remembered.

When Tommy Hodson hit Eddie Fuller on the back line of the end zone with 1:41 to play, the home crowd unleashed such a thunder that its tremor registered on a seismograph in the LSU geology building a half-mile from the football arena—and precisely at the instant those on the field felt a quake ripple across Tiger Stadium.

Verge Ausberry, now an assistant athletic director at LSU, was then a linebacker standing on the sidelines. "When Eddie caught the ball," Ausberry later said, "we could feel the vibrations under our feet, and that was the first time we had felt that."

* * *

The Tigers were pinned down most of the night by Auburn's formidable defense, so much so that LSU saw the Auburn side of the field just once before the fourth quarter.

Still, the LSU defense was playing as well as Auburn's, keeping the Tigers within hailing distance.

"Pete Jenkins [then LSU's defensive line coach] used to always preach to us that every team had one drive in it," Hodson recalled. "You see it all the time—one team really pounding another—but the team being whipped would somehow gather itself together for one drive. That wasn't a conscious thought in our minds the night of the Auburn game, but I think it was in the back of our heads."

And LSU was able to pull itself for one memorable late drive—and a very memorable Tiger victory.

LSU was coming off two straight losses that evened its record at 2-2. "But we still thought we had a pretty good team," Hodson said. "The thing was, now we had to put up or shut up."

LSU didn't have much of a case to make against undefeated Auburn until pretty late in the game. But the outcome had repercussions for the remainder of the season.

Shackled all night by the SEC's best defense, the Bayou Bengals lurched to life in the final minutes, making two unforgettable fourth down plays—including the only touchdown of the evening—to stun the nation's fourth-ranked team, handing Auburn its only defeat of the season. Ultimately, the victory knocked the Plainsmen out of any shot at the national championship. At season's end, it also gave LSU a share of the SEC championship.

* * *

LSU started the season a team on fire, easily brushing aside Texas A&M (27-0) and Tennessee (34-9); and, as noted by the national media, looking every bit the part of a No. 1 contender. Then everything came apart, starting with a horrific fourth quarter at Ohio State when the

Tommy Hodson's pass set off an earthquake-like reaction under Tiger Stadium.

Tigers unraveled and allowed two late Buckeye touchdowns in a 36-33 defeat. Then LSU lost 19-6 at Florida, a game in which the Tiger coaching staff counted 35 offensive mistakes.

The suddenly shaky Tigers now had to go against lean, mean and mighty capable Auburn and its iron defense, which featured Tracy Rocker and Craig Ogletree and had manhandled four straight opponents.

LSU—and Hodson—were in for more of the same.

* * *

Auburn spent the night either sacking or pressuring Hodson, and kept the LSU running game in check. For three and a half quarters, the Tigers couldn't penetrate the Auburn 23. Until six minutes remained, LSU's meager offensive statistics totaled 138 yards and eight first downs. The Tigers had already punted 11 times and in the first half had just 54 yards and two first downs. And yet, the LSU defense matched Auburn's offense. Only two field goals by Auburn's Win Lyle were scored going into the final period. But it seemed more than enough.

"I thought we'd win with three points," Auburn linebacker Quinton Riggins said ruefully afterward.

But after Lyle's 41-yard field goal with 10:18 to go made the score 6-0—and it really seemed like 60-0—LSU, starting at its 24 with no timeouts remaining, somehow found just enough in its offense to pull off a miracle. Hodson hit Tony Moss for 19 yards, and tight end Willie Williams made a sideline catch for a 13-yard gain to the Auburn 45— only the second time LSU crossed into Auburn's side of the field—before being rolled out of bounds.

Hodson had worked the Tigers to the 21 with 3:33 left when he went to Fuller, the 5-foot-8 fullback, who dropped the ball at the goal line. A Hodson scramble netted one yard, and the third-down pass was incomplete, setting up the play that proved to be precursor of things to come.

Hodson, on fourth-and-nine, found Williams in the flat. Williams was hit immediately but dived for three more yards to the 11, just making the first down with 2:45 to play.

"That was clutch," Hodson marveled at Williams' determination.

Hodson then speared Fuller at the back end of the end zone, but Fuller came down with one foot a millimeter out of bounds. Two straight rollout passes fell incomplete.

On fourth-and-10, as they broke the huddle, Hodson said teasingly to his diminutive fullback, "Next time, catch it." Those words must have weighed on Fuller, who, after all, had just let two touchdown passes sail through his hands.

This time, on the same play LSU ran on first down, Hodson found an open Fuller in the north end zone, this time a comfortable three yards shy of the end line.

The roar of the crowd was positively deafening.

LSU grad and PGA champion David Toms, a rabid fan who'd seen the stadium at its most raucous, said flatly: "It was the biggest roar I ever heard in Tiger Stadium."

"After Tommy and I made eye contact, he threw the ball, and I didn't hear anything or see anything except the ball," Fuller said. "Everything was in slow motion. I thought I was the only one in the stadium."

"I knew he was going to be open," Hodson said. "I saw the [line] backer lose him. ... I was praying to God he'd catch the ball. I have confidence in everybody, but if there is one man I have confidence in, it's Eddie Fuller. He'll make the big play."

Fuller, that is, and Williams. Oh, and one other Tiger: kicker David Browndyke, whose almost forgotten task was to kick the PAT—the deciding point. Browndyke hit the finger of holder Chris Mook, but the ball went through the uprights.

LSU had its improbable 7-6 victory.

The Tigers stayed in contention by playing grudging defense. Both Hodson and Fuller point to the defense as the heroes who made the victory possible. LSU yielded 316 yards to a team that had been averaging 510.

Yet 75 yards of LSU's own 213-yard total came on its last drive; six of Hodson's 17 completions came on the last drive. The Tigers gained just 28 yards rushing, and Fuller was their leading runner with 15 yards.

Tommy Hodson left LSU as the SEC's leading passer.

Assessed Hodson: "We didn't get a lot of first downs [13], a lot of completions [19-of-42], or a lot of yards rushing, but we got the most points."

* * *

Hodson left more than just the memory of one game—as exciting as it was—at LSU.

One could assert that any LSU all-star team should include Hodson on its starting unit. When he left, no one—not Y.A. Tittle, not Bert Jones—had ever quarterbacked the Tigers to as many victories (31), passed for as many yards (9,115, the SEC record at the time), threw as many completions (674), or as many touchdown passes (69). Hodson received the highest accolade from a man not given to tossing them around, from former LSU coach Bill Arnsparger—architect of some of best defenses in NFL memory at Miami—who was the athletic director at University of Florida in 1987 when the Tigers played at Georgia. Watching the televised game in the Gator press box, Arnsparger saw Hodson take a vicious cheap shot five yards out of bounds, temporarily forcing him to the bench.

"Don't worry about him," Arnsparger commented to those standing around the TV screen. "That's the toughest kid I've ever been around."

Hodson returned to throw the winning touchdown pass in a 26-23 Bayou Bengal victory.

He then went on to a six-year career in the NFL, mostly as a backup for the New England Patriots, Miami Dolphins, Dallas Cowboys, and New Orleans Saints. Today, he's in business in Baton Rouge with another former LSU quarterback, Jamie Howard. They own and operate the JTH Agency, which handles manufacturing outlets in Louisiana and Arkansas. He knows, though, what he'll always be remembered for at LSU.

"Of course," he said, "I'll never forget it, but it really is an honor to think that play will be always be remembered with some of the great plays in Tiger history."

CHAPTER **15**

BERT JONES

LSU 17 - Ole Miss 16
November 4, 1972 • Tiger Stadium

Bert Jones lashed the Tigers across the moonlit field in a frenzied gallop to the finish line, like Ben Hur and his chargers in the chariot races of ancient Rome.

Some say time literally stood still. When it came to a stop, 0:01 burned brightly from the Tiger Stadium scoreboard through the Louisiana darkness, and into the souls of the Ole Miss Rebels.

It was the night of LSU's most improbable—most *impossible*, some have argued—victory, 17-16 over the University of Mississippi. Jones, with that one second, or less, to play, flicked a pass out to tailback Brad Davis at the flag who juggled the ball but dove into the end zone to tie the game.

In the game's last 3:02, LSU had made up 80 yards, overcoming two fourth-down situations in a do-or-die drive against the revved-up Rebels—who clearly had outplayed the Tigers most of the night—to keep alive the nation's longest victory streak at 11.

"It seemed like time, apart from the clock, stopped," the late Norris Weese, the Rebel quarterback that night, recalled 20 years later. "The stadium just exploded. In slow motion, everyone seemed to jump 10 feet out of his seat. It was a memorable moment, but it wasn't a pleasant moment."

Actually, it was—for LSU partisans. Harry Harrison, who hit Davis as the Tiger back went over the goal-line pylon, argued that Davis never had control of the ball, and that he frequently dreams of that play. Except that, in his dreams, he intercepts and runs 95 yards for a touchdown.

Rebel proponents from that day to today contend that LSU benefited from faulty time-keeping, citing the impossibility of getting off three plays in the final 10 seconds.

Actually, the controversy centers on one play, not three. With 10 seconds left, interference was called on Ole Miss, stopping the clock with four seconds to play and putting the Tigers at the Rebel 10.

After the next pass was broken up, the one disputed second remained. The time remaining on LSU's last play, the touchdown, was inconsequential because, obviously, a play cannot end while in progress. Whether the game should have ended on the second-to-last play is the crux of the matter—very few arguments claim the pass took more than four seconds. Because the electric clock runs on tenths of a second, though, LSU may have been working with a hair under five seconds, not four.

James W. Campbell Jr. of Memphis was the electric-clock operator that night, and he admitted years later the last few plays of that series were handled differently than usual. The clock operator usually stands at the line of scrimmage where he activates a stopped clock at the snap of the ball. But for some reason, perhaps someone standing on the wire, the cord did not reach the line of scrimmage on the last few plays. Campbell said he was trying to see through the feet of the quarterback and center to catch the precise instant of the snap, but couldn't. He started the clock at the first movement of the quarterback.

SEC commissioner Boyd McWhorter attended and said he didn't even realize there was a controversy until he returned to Birmingham the next day.

"I didn't question it at the time," McWhorter said. "I was like everyone else, caught up in the excitement of a thrilling game."

SEC Supervisor of Officials George Gardner brought the film to Georgia Tech and broke it down frame by frame. The SEC could not find fault with Campbell.

With one second remaining, Bert Jones flicks the winning touchdown pass.

New Orleans sportscaster Buddy Diliberto, with a reputation of fair and independent journalism, had his television station engineers break down the film, too. They also could not find Campbell in error for what was obviously a hairline call.

* * *

Jones was a consolation prize, a gawky kid with mussed fawn-colored hair and a big-toothed grin. He became, however, one of the biggest basement bargains in LSU annals.

He walked onto the Louisiana State University campus in 1969 as the unheralded afterthought of a recruiting TKO. From there Jones went on to quarterback the Tigers to 27 victories in a 36-game career, would stamp his signature throughout the school's offensive record book, and would be considered by panting professionals as the rightful heir to Johnny Unitas.

No doubt in Jones' own mind he disputed he was a supreme talent; but nearly everyone was dazzled by the polished poise of another north Louisiana quarterback, Joe Ferguson.

Ferguson, of Shreveport-Woodlawn, amassed awesome statistics directing a pro-style offense; while Jones, still growing into his 6-foot-3 frame, labored for Ruston High, which ran a conservative offense. Every coach in the South, and even beyond, wanted Ferguson. Louisiana Tech, Tulane, and Grambling showed the most interest in Jones.

Grambling coach Eddie Robinson—who noted that Bert's father, Dub, had played and coached at Cleveland and that Bert's youth was spent pestering Frank Ryan and Jim Ninowski for football tips—asked: "How could he miss? He was watching films of his dad running pass routes when other kids were watching cartoons."

When Gov. John McKeithen and Y.A. Tittle were trying to woo Ferguson to LSU, the Tigers made a cursory offer of a grant-in-aid to Jones, projecting him as a backup, no doubt. Intelligent and realistic, Jones realized no school would have room for both and waited for Ferguson to make his choice. When Ferguson signed with Arkansas, Jones signed with LSU.

What Bert and Dub both knew—but what others had to be shown when he reported to LSU as a freshman—quickly became apparent on the practice field: this young prospect could hurl thunderbolts. He had the confidence of a champion, which his teammates loved, and he was as headstrong as he was talented, which bothered his coaches.

Jones spent a lot of time in McClendon's doghouse, and eventually found himself backing up converted cornerback Paul Lyons, who was 5-foot-10, 190 pounds, and possessed nothing close to Jones' natural ability. He did run the option very well, however—no small inducement in McClendon's run-oriented offense—and the team responded to Lyons.

"He knew the game, all right," confided one of Jones' teammates, "but not as thoroughly as he thought he did. He didn't accept advice easily. I think it was pretty hard on him, especially when he saw how the team reacted to Paul Lyons. What made it hard—Bert realized as everyone else did—was there was no comparison between his athletic ability and Paul's. [But] This was college, not the pros."

No one knew it at the time, but the unhappy Jones was contemplating a transfer. He never did, but later said he felt his talents were never completely utilized in Baton Rouge. "I probably threw more third-down passes than any man in history," Jones said later, "but never a first-down pass." Acknowledging that McClendon also had excellent qualities as a coach, Jones also reflected, "There were just some things that, all things being equal, I would have done differently."

But he decided against transferring—and became an All-America quarterback, the only one LSU had ever produced.

Against Notre Dame in 1971, Jones' junior season, McClendon, noting the height difference between Jones and Lyons, and the size of the Irish defensive line, started Jones. After a 28-8 thumping in which Jones went 7-for-9 for 143 yards and figured in three touchdowns, Bert never again backed up another player. In that season's final three games, including a Sun Bowl appearance, Jones threw eight touchdown passes and completed 30 of his 46 attempts.

"I had a lot of games people remember, Notre Dame, Auburn, some others," Jones, now owner of a lumber-preservation business in Simsboro, Louisiana. "But if you ask the average guy on the street, that Ole Miss game is the one they all remember."

* * *

The loose Rebels, playing only for pride in a disappointing season, turned the Tigers every which way but out for 57 minutes. A missed field goal that would have given Ole Miss an insurmountable 19-10 lead with three minutes remaining allowed Jones to breathe life into the listless Bayou Bengals.

"We were in a position where we had to throw," Jones mused, "and we did."

He certainly did, in a remarkable, frenzied race against the clock, Jones jockeyed his team steadily up-field on a series of short and medium

Bert Jones stamped his imprint on Tiger record books.

darters to his backs, taking whatever the defense would yield until 70 of the necessary 80 yards were gained.

The interference penalty gave LSU new life, but the only controversy Jones said he was aware of when he looked up and saw one second remaining was that the refs missed a call.

"They interfered again," Jones said, "and got away with it."

During a timeout called by Ole Miss, McClendon said he told his quarterback, "Bert, this is what you came to LSU for." Jones winked and trotted back out to pull off his most memorable feat as a Tiger.

The horn went off with the snap on the game's last play. Jones flipped the ball to Davis, a running back, who bobbled the ball, then wheeled into the end zone.

Rusty Jackson's conversion was delayed several minutes because of the pandemonium. When he did kick it, the game became a Tiger landmark: the first time since Dr. Charles Coates introduced football at LSU in 1893 that a game was decided with no time remaining on the game clock.

Days after the LSU-Ole Miss game, a sign went up on the Louisiana-Mississippi border with the inscription: "Entering Louisiana, set your clocks back four seconds."

The next year the score in the Rebel football media guide read: "Ole Miss 16, LSU 10, plus 7." The Bayou Bengals got even a year later, after a 51-14 waxing of the Rebels. *The Daily Reveille*, the LSU school paper, ran the score as: "Ole Miss 14, LSU 10, plus 7, plus 7, plus 7, plus 7, plus 7, plus 6."

CHAPTER 16

JERRY JOSEPH

LSU 14 - Arkansas 7
Jan. 1, 1966 • Dallas, Texas

The ball whizzed past Jerry Joseph's fingertips—and into the arms of Arkansas All-America receiver Bobby Crockett, who had run a down-and-out.

"He caught it around the 15, and there I was laying on the sideline watching him tightrope his way into the end zone. It was not a good feeling," Joseph recalled decades after the fact.

Things were not starting out well for LSU, just as all reasonable football prognosticators were expecting for this 1966 Cotton Bowl between the national-title challenger Razorbacks—ranked No. 2 and riding a 22-game victory streak—and the very disappointing 7-3 Bayou Bengals. On its second possession, Arkansas drove 87 yards for that touchdown, and the rout was seemingly on.

Joseph, who weighed in at 5-feet-10, 175 pounds, had the assignment of taking Crockett in LSU's man-to-man scheme. "I went back to our secondary coach, Bill Beall, and told him, 'I can't handle this guy by myself, it's just not possible. This guy is just too good,'" Joseph, then a 19-year-old junior, said.

Beall immediately said LSU would go to another perimeter defense, one that would "bracket" Crockett. The concept was something the

Tigers tried sparingly but experimented with in practice. Joseph would still have Crockett, but he would "follow" the receiver in his routes instead of trying to stay with him step for step.

"As soon as the receiver turned," Joseph said, "you turned."

In theory, he would be in position to make a defensive play. If that didn't work, a safety, Sammy Grezaffi—a track sprinter and LSU's fastest football player—was also playing behind the pair to prevent a major gain in case a catch was still made. Joseph felt better, though he still realized he'd be under the gun all afternoon.

* * *

In those days, Arkansas was a member of the Southwest Conference, whose champion hosted the Cotton Bowl annually. The Razorbacks hadn't lost in two seasons; in fact, the Hogs were defending national champions of the United Press International's coaches' poll and had a golden opportunity to add to their growing list of football accolades.

Conversely, the question everywhere had to be: "What in the heck was thrice-beaten LSU doing in Dallas on New Year's Day anyway?"

The answer was Tiger AD Jim Corbett, a master of persuasion, who was well aware of how nervous the Cotton Bowl was about its most logical choice for its visiting spot. After it became apparent that third-ranked Nebraska was going to the Orange Bowl to play Alabama, Dallas looked to Tennessee. The Vols were 6-1-2 but still had a late game with UCLA, so Corbett sold the Cotton Bowl selection committee on LSU.

Suddenly, the disappointing Tigers—who opened the season with a No. 8 ranking and rose as high as No. 5 before a series of crippling injuries at quarterback—were in a major bowl against a major, major opponent. Arkansas led the nation in scoring at 32.4 points per game and their running tandem of Harry Jones and Bobby Burnett averaged 7.7 yards per carry.

Razorbacks head coach Frank Broyles couldn't have been happy to be paired against an underachieving opponent, in which a victory would prove nothing. But a late decision by The Associated Press took away what should have been a psychological disadvantage for Broyles' team.

Jerry Joseph made a crucial play in an exhilarating Cotton Bowl victory.

For the first time, the news organization decided to take a final poll after the bowls. The reason was three undefeated teams—No. 1-ranked Michigan State, No.2 Arkansas, and No. 3 Nebraska, all with legitimate arguments for the 'national championship.' The unbeaten, untied Razorbacks of 1965 already claimed the No. 1 tag of the Football Writers of America Association, but the more recognized wire service title would validate Arkansas' football achievements of the mid-1960s.

LSU, though, was flying under the radar. The hobbled and re-cobbled Tigers had talent, evidenced by producing four future pros, including All-America tackle George Rice and flanker Doug Moreau.

Sophomore quarterback Nelson Stokely got off to a spectacular start in 1965 before falling to a knee injury. Backup Pat Screen had to fill in and, at first, showed his rust.

"We were just deflated," said Moreau. "We couldn't seem to hit all cylinders."

Broyles said then and now: "LSU was every bit as good as we were when they were healthy. They were a great team until they had those injuries at quarterback."

Pat Screen, who started the two previous seasons before shoulder and knee injuries short-circuited what could have been a sterling college career, steered LSU past Mississippi State (37-20) and Tulane (62-0).

"Pat was picking up from where he was before," Moreau said. "At the end of the season, we were a pretty good football team again."

Even Tiger coach Charlie McClendon wasn't quite as frightened as outsiders suspected. He was well aware that anything less than a perfect game plan—and execution—could result in humiliation. LSU, a nine-point underdog, practiced a month with the scout squad all wearing the number "23," the implications being obvious. The Tigers did not want to end the year as merely the latest Razorbacks victim. But McClendon also knew his team was not a sacrificial lamb, and that LSU really had a chance. In fact, the coach privately felt he just might present the best rushing offense the Razorbacks had seem. Lost in Arkansas' gaudy record—but not to the LSU coaching staff—was this interesting tidbit: the Hogs surrendered more than 400 yards in somehow beating run-oriented Texas 27-24 during the regular season.

A healthy LSU, Mac knew, had more than a chance.

Not every one was that perceptive—and to McClendon's delight, fans and media played right into his hands. When LSU got to Dallas, the Hog faithful made a point of mocking the Tigers with the smirking question, "LS-Who?" Moreau recalled hearing a reporter ask the Tigers' coach, "How bad do you expect your team to lose?"

"You know, there's a lot of arrogance in a question like that," Moreau said 30 years after the fact. "It makes you angry, and we were focused. We wanted to show we belonged. At the same time, it also scared us, because if they were that good, we'd have to play our very best game just to be respectable."

As the Tigers left the hotel for the buses that would take them to the Cotton Bowl, a little old woman wearing one of those silly red Porker hats in the lobby shrieked at the sight: "Look, they're actually going to show up."

* * *

They didn't seem present at first. The Razorbacks came out sharp and surgically sliced up the Tigers on the series in which Crockett victimized Joseph, tiptoeing 16 yards down the sideline. Another Hog drive ended with a missed field goal, though, and LSU didn't fold. Cold water had been thrown in their faces, and the Tigers readjusted. Screen guided the Tiger offense, which had a slightly different look from the one Broyles studied on film. Joe Labruzzo, a dangerous 5-foot-9, 170-pound tailback, was lined up deeper than usual so he could pick his options on the fly, depending on how the Razorbacks lined up. The Bengal offensive line began taking control, blowing the defense off the ball. Labruzzo cut back behind the blocks of 6-foot-5 Billy Masters and 6-foot-6 tackle Dave McCormick.

Perhaps as an indication that fate was finally going to smile on the '65 Tigers, LSU got a monumental break when Screen, playing a second-and-16 from midfield, called a pass to Masters. Razorback Tommy Sain reached out and tipped the pass. After spinning around, he had control for a second, but the ball flew out and into the grasp of Masters, who turned it into a 14-yard gain.

Nine plays later, the score was 7-7, LSU impressively going 80 yards in 16 plays with Labruzzo scoring from the 3. After recovering a fumble at Arkansas' 34, Screen continued to hammer the Hogs with body-blow plays. Rejecting a call from the bench once LSU reached the 19, Screen ran Labruzzo five straight times at left tackle. With 18 seconds remaining until the half, Labruzzo scored again, this time from the 1-yard line.

LSU held a stunning 14-7 lead—and just as important, the emotional barometer of the Tigers was changed. They weren't just trying to stay with Arkansas any more. They smelled blood.

Assistant Doug Hamley said he never experienced anything like the halftime of that game. "We couldn't hold the team in the dressing room," Hamley said. "They got up four times and tried to leave, but Coach McClendon had to hold them back because the bands were still on the field."

Bill Beall later pointed to marks on the floor describing the way those caged Tigers pawed at the concrete as they waited for the halftime show to end.

"I knew they were ready," McClendon said. "That is, I felt if this team wasn't ready to play, I could never be sure of any team in the future."

They were. LSU made the halftime score hold up with a string of stirring defensive stands, once stopping the Hogs on the Tiger 15, where they missed a field goal. Moreau, who set a national record with 14 field goals in 1964, also missed a short one that could have given LSU a bit more space—which could have been crucial because Arkansas cranked up another threatening drive from its 20 that went to the LSU 36.

At that point, Razorback quarterback Jon Brittenum put the ball up for Crockett.

"I was guarding him on the outside," Joseph remembered, "and he got by me, so I started 'following' him—running right behind him. When he turned, I turned and … the truth of the matter is, the ball just hit me in the hands. It was like a dart. It was 100 percent instinct. I had no time to think. All of a sudden there was the ball, and I caught it."

LSU had the ball back at its 20 with 4:38 to play. The Tigers didn't run out the clock, but by blunting that drive, they seemed to take the remaining air out of the Razorbacks' sails.

Broyles called the interception the turning point of the game, adding that, until Joseph made the pick, he still believed Arkansas would win. He also said that, in his long and distinguished career, "It's the sickest I've ever been in coaching."

* * *

It was a heartwarming day for LSU, but it really was heartbreaking for Broyles. That same afternoon, UCLA beat Michigan State in the Rose Bowl, meaning the Razorbacks would have been No. 1 by beating the Tigers. In the final poll, LSU finished right where it started, No. 8. No one could take anything away from LSU, though. At game's end, a sportswriter in the press box who had covered the Razorbacks throughout their long win streak commented: "I think if you study this game carefully, you'll find that LSU has played a perfect game against Arkansas."

A dejected Broyles couldn't disagree. Sitting on an equipment pile, running his fingers through his hair, he said simply: "They just beat us."

Following the landmark upset, in the euphoric LSU locker room, the still hyped-up Tigers tore a red jersey bearing No. 23 to shreds before Charlie Mac, who stood on a trunk to be heard over his whooping and hollerin' players, quieted them, and surely told them something they'd already suspected.

"The rest of your lives," Mac told them, "you won't ever forget what you did today."

Joseph didn't exactly shut down Crockett, who finished with 10 receptions for 129 yards—seven after the first quarter—but did keep him contained while waiting to spring the trap. Joseph said Mac was right, and the moment he watched the clock wind down to 0:00 remains one of the highlights of his life.

"When we were at full strength, we were a very good football team," Joseph, now a physician in Ozark, Missouri, said. "If we played that same Arkansas team 20 times, though, we might only win once. Fortunately, we only played them that once."

CHAPTER 17

KEN KAVANAUGH

LSU 26 - Holy Cross 7
October 7, 1939 • Worcester, Massachusetts

Between the steady drone of the engines and an occasional peek at the countryside 10,000 feet below, Ken Kavanaugh was fidgety.

"I was trying to figure out how they kept that big machine in the air," Kavanaugh said of that historic trip.

LSU was on its way to Worcester, Massachusetts, just outside of Boston, as one of the first college football teams to fly to a game—certainly from the South. The 37-man Tiger squad, coaches, support staff, and equipment were being ferried on the 11-hour, four-stop journey on two DC-3s to play Eastern power Holy Cross. Several of the party became airsick. "I wasn't sick," Kavanaugh, then a senior end, insisted. "I was just nervous."

Things weren't made any easier by Dave Bartram, a senior guard who was majoring in engineering. Sitting next to Coach Bernie Moore, Bartram started working out equations with his slide ruler. Moore, also jumpy, asked what he was doing. Bertram looked up, smiled, and explained, "Coach, I've just figured out that, if the engines quit, it will take us 32 seconds to hit the ground."

Ken Kavanaugh makes a catch for one of his four touchdowns against Holy Cross.

If the Tigers were going to crash into anything, the chances were it would be the Crusaders—a team that in the previous five seasons had a 40-5-4 record against the cream of the East, including: Harvard, Yale, Princeton, Fordham, Carnegie Tech, Temple, Colgate, Boston College, and Brown. The Crusaders even beat Georgia twice in the last two years; which, of course, made Holy Cross a measuring stick for the Tigers.

Holy Cross represented a major challenge to LSU, which is why the Tigers dropped the University of Texas, a team they'd beaten three straight years, from the schedule to start a series with the Crusaders.

Holy Cross Coach Joe Sheeketski seems to have agreed strictly to fatten his won-loss record. Showing no respect for his opponent before they played, Sheeketski sniffed this game would be little more than a scrimmage for his squad and that he just might start his second string against LSU.

"They laughed at us," Kavanaugh remembered. "They were asking us what we made the trip for."

* * *

Sheeketski soon realized Holy Cross had a game on its hands—but it took LSU fans a while to reach the same conclusion.

Sophomore tailback Leo Bird got off a 66-yard quick-kick that went out of bounds two inches from the Crusader goal line. When Holy Cross punted out, LSU was in business at the Crusader 32. After picking up a first down, on third-and-11 from the 22, Kavanaugh faked to the outside and shot downfield before cutting back to the inside to look back in time to Bird's high pass coming toward him.

At that very instant, the transmission of the radio broadcast was severed. The telephone line carrying the play-by-play was disconnected somewhere.

Twenty minutes later, when the broadcast resumed, listeners found out what the dismayed crowd witnessed: Kavanangh, with a high leap, took the ball right out of the hands of a safety and spun into the end zone for the first touchdown. The PAT was missed, but LSU was on the board.

The Tigers threatened again in the second quarter. Leading Kavanaugh, Bird fired a shot toward the corner of the end zone, and again a defender had a chance at the ball. As the defensive back reached high for the ball, Kavanaugh stretched his frame as far as it would stretch, made the catch, and stepped across the goal line. LSU again missed the conversion.

The onslaught continued. With LSU at the Holy Cross 15 in the third period, Kavanaugh ran straight at a linebacker, then spun directly in front of him. Bird's pass hit Kavanaugh right in the chest for his third touchdown.

Then came the score fans most remembered of that day: the Crusaders finally showed some signs of life, driving inside the LSU 15. The Tiger defense, though, strung out a wide option play, and the ball-carrier, about to go down, tried to lateral to another back. The ball seemed to hang weightless for an instant, then Kavanaugh picked it off and brought it back 74 yards for LSU's last touchdown.

Twenty-seven thousand Holy Cross fans sat in stunned silence.

Headlines in the country's major papers heralded the story.

The New York Times read:
Louisiana Upsets Holy Cross, 26-7
Kavanaugh Scores Four Tiger Touchdowns, Going 74 Yards on Intercepted Lateral

The Boston Post wrote:
H.C. Walloped by Louisiana State, 26-7
Ken Kavanaugh, Giant End, Hero of Colossal Gridiron Upset

The Worchester Sunday Telegram said:
Louisiana Routs Holy Cross in Stunning Grid Upset, 26-7
Kavanaugh Makes All Four Scores

* * *

The returned lateral wasn't the first of its kind for Kavanaugh, who stood 6 feet 3, 200 pounds—a big man for the day. In one of the most storied single plays in LSU history, against Rice in 1937, the Owls drove inside the Tiger 1. As ball-carrier Red Vickers hit the line, he was smacked hard, and the ball went flying out of his arms. Kavanaugh grabbed it with one foot in the end zone, one out. He took off and didn't stop for 100 yards, the biggest play in a 13-0 LSU victory.

In 1939, when Kavanaugh led the nation in receptions with 30 for 531 yards, he shared the SEC MVP with Tennessee's Bobby Foxx. Kavanaugh, who scored seven consecutive touchdowns—still an LSU record—also won the Knute Rockne Memorial Award as the year's outstanding lineman and finished seventh in the Heisman Trophy balloting. He was the barometer by which LSU receivers were measured for decades. "Kavanaugh was a pass completer rather than receiver," Coach Bernie Moore said, "simply because he'd catch passes no one else could get to."

An All-American, Kavanaugh said his Holy Cross game was responsible more than any other single factor.

"It was everything," Kavanaugh said. "It was played in the East, where the most influential sportswriters could see us. They really didn't know the quality of players and teams elsewhere in the country. We had a good game, and they were impressed."

* * *

Kavanaugh went on to a varied career as an All-Pro receiver with the Chicago Bears, and he still holds the NFL record for most touchdowns per catch (162 receptions, 50 TDs). He is on the Bears' all-time team as well. During his 60-year pro football career as a player, coach, and scout, Kavanaugh was a part of six NFL World Championships, including two Super Bowls.

Flying 30 missions in B-24s and B-17s over Germany during World War II, Kavanaugh received the Distinguished Flying Cross for "Extraordinary achievement while serving as commander in the air squadron formations on heavy bombardment missions against the enemy." It was an ironic development, considering his queasiness while flying to Holy Cross a few years earlier.

His off-season careers included cattle ranching in the Sierra Nevada mountains, and a lumber and fuel business in Philadelphia.

Ken Kavanaugh Jr., who grew up in Pennsylvania as his father worked as a coach and scout in professional football, followed his daddy to LSU, where he played on some outstanding teams in the late '60s and early '70s as a split end. Ken Jr. chronicled Ken Sr.'s life story in a book, *The Greatness of Humility: The Adventures of a WWII Hero and NFL Legend.*

But had Kavanaugh never caught a pass, he still would have left an imprint on LSU. He played a role in securing Mike, LSU's beloved Bengal tiger mascot.

The idea came in 1936 from W.G. "Hickey" Higginbotham, LSU's swim coach, author of one of the Tiger fight songs and a former school cheerleader. He thought a mascot could be purchased strictly from student donations. LSU's 250-pound athletic trainer, Mike Chambers—a man who once blocked for Red Grange at the University of Illinois and one of the most popular figures on the Tiger campus—immediately began a nationwide search for an available animal at a reasonable price.

As it happened, Kavanaugh gave Tiger tradition an assist by writing his mother back home in Little Rock, Arkansas.

"I asked her to check out the Little Rock zoo to see if any tigers might be for sale," Kavanaugh said. "Sure enough, there were two, one priced at $500, another at $750."

Kavanaugh relayed the news to Chambers and, presto, there were signs posted all over the university, requesting each student to contribute 25 cents in the fund-raising drive that was confined exclusively to the student body.

"In those days," Kavanaugh reminded, "a quarter was enough to buy you dinner. It was a lot to ask of a student. But football fever was running so high—we were conference champions in '36—contributions came to almost $1,000. Which meant we had enough to buy the $750 tiger."

Mike the Tiger was named for Chambers, and he and his descendants have ruled over LSU sports ever since.

Ken Kavanaugh led the nation in 1939 with 30 receptions.

CHAPTER 18

TODD KINCHEN

LSU 17 - Texas A&M 8
September 29, 1990 • Tiger Stadium

He had similar exploits many times—in his imagination.

"After all we went through at practice, I used to run afterward," Todd Kinchen said. "I'd run and run and run, and when I reached the point of exhaustion, in order to keep going, I'd think of plays, what I'd do in our next game, how I'd cut back and get away from a defender, or pull away from a pack of tacklers. My imagination would take my mind off my fatigue and give me the energy to keep going."

In due time, against 11th-ranked Texas A&M in the fourth game of the 1990 season, Kinchen's fantasies became stark reality for the Aggies, 17-8.

"It was as spectacular a performance as anyone ever turned in around here," LSU associate athletic director Herb Vincent said, very mindful of the plethora of football feats by LSU Tigers through the decades.

Kinchen, then a junior split end and kick returner, electified Tiger Stadium with two dazzling dashes in a span of 1:23 of the fourth quarter to ignite the upset of an A&M squad that had outscored its first three opponents by an average of 43-11. On top of that, LSU was still red-faced a week after an exasperating upset of its own, 24-21 to

Vanderbilt—a defeat in which Kinchen had a game-winning catch nullified when he was called for pushing off a defender.

"That was a disappointment," Kinchen recalled, remembering that he also dropped a pass that would have been a touchdown against Vandy. "But it really wasn't on my mind against A&M. All I did was play hard, just as I did against Vanderbilt. I just dedicated the A&M game to the Lord, and I think He blessed me."

Who could disagree? Kinchen delivered in a head-turning performance, taking a swing pass into a meandering 79-yard touchdown, then returning a punt 60 yards to set up LSU's clinching points. Kinchen, an All-SEC receiver, had several notable games in his time at Tiger Town.

But this was the game of his daydreams.

* * *

Kinchen was born to be a Tiger. So were his brother, Brian; his father, Gaynell, and his uncle, Gary. An older brother, Cal, may have been the best athlete of the bunch, according to Todd—and although he did get his business degree from LSU, Cal didn't play college ball.

His mother, Toni, was not only an LSU cheerleader for four years, but twice reigned at homecoming as the Darling of LSU. That caused the rules for homecoming royalty being changed, according to Todd:

"After that, it was decided that you could only be the queen once. Without that change, from what I understand, my mom might have been the Darling of LSU for four straight years."

Get the drift? It wouldn't be a stretch to think of the Kinchens as the First Family of LSU football.

"I was hearing about LSU football as long as I can remember, since I was a child," Todd recalled. "Our family was such a part of it, and my dad and uncle shared their stories with us."

They were colorful—and true—tales.

Gaynell "Gus" Kinchen was named for Gaynell "Gus" Tinsley, LSU's coach in the late 1940s and early '50s. "My parents were big fans [of his namesake, a '30s Tiger All-America end]," Gaynell said.

Todd Kinchen electrified Tiger Stadium against the Aggies.

By the mid-'50s, Gaynell was a member of the LSU football team—though in 1957 it was as a team manager, courtesy of a knee injury. Later, it was as a member of LSU's famed defensive unit, the Chinese Bandits—on the '58 No. 1 team through 1960—making some of the Tigers' biggest plays of the era. He recovered the Ole Miss fumble that led to the Tigers' first touchdown in the 14-0 victory in 1958. Then, two years later in Oxford, when LSU was a three-touchdown underdog, Kinchen helped foil the Rebels' perfect season and national championship aspirations in a 6-6 tie with a timely sack of quarterback Jake Gibbs.

Gus' brother, Gary, played center for the Tigers from 1960 through 1962; anchoring teams that lost just two games in his last two seasons.

Twenty-four years after his last game in a Tiger uniform, Gus' son, Brian, started his LSU career. Brian became an All-SEC tight end, whose late touchdown catch of a Tommy Hodson pass gave LSU a thrilling 26-23 nod over Georgia in 1987.

Then came Todd. "I had a lot of offers [to play at other major schools] when I played at Trafton Academy in Baton Rouge," he recalled. "But I didn't even make a trip [to other campuses]. I knew where I wanted to go, and LSU wanted me, too. I just figured I'd be wasting their time and mine."

It was like Todd was stepping into the huge Bayou Bengal footprints of the Kinchens who had gone before him. Eventually, he entered LSU lore with his breathtaking 79-yard run against Texas A&M, which had wide-eyed fans comparing it to Billy Cannon's storied run against Ole Miss 31 years before.

* * *

Chad Loup, making his first start at quarterback, found himself staring at a third-and-9 at the LSU 21, with the Tigers hanging on to a 3-0 lead midway through the last quarter. Loup flipped the ball to Kinchen, who, crossing over the middle, slipped free from a pack of Aggies, got to the left sidelines, and set sail up field. Cornerback Kevin Smith tried to corner him at the A&M 35, but Kinchen spun to his right then headed diagonally across the field, a run that ended with him diving into the end zone.

"If you asked me to tell you what I did, or why, I couldn't tell you," Kinchen said. "I know I was surprised because Smith was right on me, and he was a pretty fast guy. Somehow I got away, but there was no design or thought involved in that run. It was nothing but pure instinct."

The pyrotechnics weren't over. When A&M failed to move the ball on its next possession, the Aggies kicked. Big mistake. Kinchen said he was "still sucking air" after what seemed to be his just-completed touchdown jaunt.

"I was thinking of a fair-catch," Kinchen said. "But, you know, once the ball's in the air I always wanted to try to run it back."

A&M made the decision easy by kicking a line-drive punt. Kinchen took the ball at his 17, shot up the middle, and then found a seam on the left sidelines. Picking up speed as he crossed midfield, Kinchen looked to be on his way to another touchdown when Dennis Ransom pulled him down from behind at the A&M 23.

"That's exactly what he looked like on film," A&M linebacker William Thomas said. "We just needed for someone to hit him and hold on to him."

Kinchen's explanation was: "All I did was follow my blockers. I followed the purple and gold." Six plays later, the Tigers scored their second touchdown, expanding their lead to 17-0 with 7:26 remaining. A&M eventually scored to avert the shutout, but for 51 minutes, the LSU defense shut down the nation's third-ranked offense to provide the stage for Kinchen's effulgent show—ultimately the difference between the football foes.

* * *

There was a third stirring breakaway by Kinchen that night, though it didn't show up in the stat sheet. In the first half, with LSU at its 36, Kinchen took a short pass from Loup near the right sidelines, dodged a couple of defenders and dashed across the field, outrunning almost the whole Aggie team until he was knocked out of bounds at the A&M 5 by Smith.

"The thing I remember about that, more than anything," Kinchen said, "was the block [tailback] Odell Beckham threw for me. He blocked

Todd Kinchen (49) breaks loose against Texas A&M.

a guy near midfield, hit him perfectly, and that guy went completely head over heels. It was in the open, and the crowd saw; and I remember their roar."

He also remembers the groan of the crowd when what would have been a 59-yard gain was brought back 40 yards because of a clip. The run netted only 19 yards, to the A&M 45, and LSU never did score. Still, Kinchen left a lasting memory against Texas A&M, finishing the night with five receptions for 133 yards and a touchdown, and returned two kicks for 85 yards and a touchdown.

* * *

Todd and Brian both went on to play in the NFL, with Todd putting in eight years with the Los Angeles Rams, Denver Broncos, and Atlanta Falcons. He and his dad are now back on the same team—Gus ministers to the Baton Rouge-area Fellowship of Christian Athletes (FCA), and Todd is an FCA field representative for the region's high schools and for LSU. The job keeps him very busy—almost as busy as spending time with his own family, centered on his three little daughters.

"Yeah," he said, "they're little Tigers too; but I guess they'll be softball or volleyball Tigers, or maybe Tiger cheerleaders, like their grandma."

* * *

Texas A&M is hard to forget for LSU fans in the early '90s. It was a brilliant individual performance by an athlete playing on a sub-par team (5-6) against a better-than-average opponent. The Aggies would finish 9-3-1. It wasn't, however, Kinchen's most productive game. A year later, against Mississippi State, he caught nine passes for what was then an LSU-record 248 yards.

"They were both pretty special to me," Kinchen said. "A&M meant something because the Aggies were so good; we were struggling, and we really had to get up to play with them. What happened after that is hard to imagine—except for some kid with football dreams."

CHAPTER 19

KENNY KONZ

LSU 21 - Tulane 0
November 26, 1949 • New Orleans, Louisiana

It was an incredible sight—and prediction. Painted on a runway in the south end of Tulane Stadium was the lettering: LSU 21, TU 0.

A three-column picture of the mad forecast wound up on page one of New Orleans' morning newspaper, *The Times-Picayune*, above a story saying some LSU students, under cover of darkness, also had stolen into Tulane Stadium and used rock salt to burn the letters "L-S-U" into the turf between the 30-yard lines.

It was a time for football prophets. As the skittish Tigers prepared in Baton Rouge for their invasion of Tulane, LSU coach Gaynell Tinsley, watching Kenny Konz boom punt after punt into the stratosphere, was moved to exclaim, "Kenny, you could win this game all by yourself!" Konz had caught Tinsley's eye with a week of exceptional practice, on offense, defense, and special teams as the Tigers prepared for their traditional regular-season finale against archrival Tulane. A half-century later, though, Konz remembered thinking, "That is ridiculous. Nobody is going to beat this team alone." There was no certainty that, even if every member of the 1949 Tiger team played his best game, LSU could win, Konz later admitted.

Both predictions came to pass, but against all reason.

* * *

The Green Wave was not only the already crowned Southeastern Conference champion, it was a powerhouse that humiliated LSU in 1948 by what was then the largest margin in the ancient series, an embarrassing 46-0.

Tulane had been a preseason No. 1 pick by *The Sporting News* and a universal Top-10 selection. Any aspirations the Wave had of winning the national championship disappeared with a 46-7 thumping by Notre Dame in South Bend. To its credit, Tulane picked itself up and, other than a tie with Navy, put itself back into the college football elite, winning the SEC, securing a No. 10 ranking with a 7-1-1 record, and was ready to accept a Sugar Bowl invitation with a victory over LSU.

On the other hand, LSU, a seven-point underdog, wasn't exactly in uncharted waters.

The Tigers were in the midst of what would forevermore be called their "Cinderella" season, an almost magical ride in which LSU became America's most publicized football "David."

Coming off a horrendous 1948 in which the Bayou Bengals were 3-7, LSU lost two of its first four games before coming on to defeat three conference champions (Rice of the Southwest Conference, 14-7, North Carolina of the Southern Conference, 13-7, and Tulane) for a 7-2 record and a No. 13 national ranking.

The turnabout was so stunning that only a quick comparison with '48 can correctly place it in focus. The Tigers were outscored 186-33 in five 1948 defeats (North Carolina, Ole Miss, Vanderbilt, Mississippi State, and Tulane). In 1949, LSU outscored those same five teams 136-34, defeating each.

On top of that, there was something other than pride to play for, though it also was a long-shot possibility. At that time, the Sugar Bowl was an "open bowl"—meaning it could take whoever it wanted and whoever wanted it, not necessarily the SEC champion. The SEC then had a rule stipulating its members had to have a .750 winning percentage in conference games to play in a bowl. A victory would give LSU a 4-2 league record (.667).

A football jack-of-all-trades was LSU's Kenny Konz.

* * *

"Where did that No. 22 come from?" the stunned Green Wave would wonder.

A jack of all trades, Konz put in time at safety, cornerback, quarterback, fullback, and end. He kicked off, kicked extra points, punted, and returned punts. Konz, who was 5-feet-10, 185 pounds, ran the 100 in 9.9—noteworthy for the time. After leaving his mark on college football as a senior, he would be described as "The SEC's All-Around Best" by The Associated Press.

"He's one of those special men who have made LSU football what it is," said John Ferguson, longtime voice of the Tigers who saw Konz play. "Kenny wasn't a big man, but he had a lot of ability, and he played with a big heart."

Before matriculating to LSU, Konz had only played six-man football at Weimar High School (Texas). A fan from Baton Rouge named Rubin Moss used to hunt deer near Weimar, and would take in local games. Moss was impressed with Konz' speed and skills, as anyone would have been. Konz scored 120 career touchdowns and passed for 40 more. He rushed for over 8,000 yards, passed for 3,800, kicked 160 PATs, and averaged 44.6 yards per punt.

Moss eagerly told the Tiger coaching staff about him.

"I had offers from just about every school in Texas," Konz said. "Six-man football is not 11-man football, but it does require quickness and skill, and I was a good athlete. They could see that.

"But my brother attended Texas A&M, and he was home every weekend, fiddlin' around, not doing his schoolwork. And all those schools were within easy driving distance. I wanted to go someplace where I was really away from home—but not so far that I couldn't get back quickly if my family needed me. LSU fit the bill."

Ferguson, along with sports information director Jim Corbett, was present at Don Lee's Restaurant on Baton Rouge's Third Street when then-coach Bernie Moore mulled over the pros and cons of giving a scholarship to a kid who had only played six-man football. "He finally decided to take a chance," Ferguson said. "The rest is history."

Tiger assistant Art Swanson called Konz, informed him that LSU had a spot for him and to get on over. "I had to hitchhike to Baton Rouge," Konz said. "But it was certainly worth it."

The lone member of 31 freshmen to make the varsity, Konz made his presence felt immediately in practice by running back a punt against the Tigers' first string. The angry coaches ran the return over again, and Konz again ran the kick back ... then a third time. LSU coaches were mad, and the first-string varsity embarrassed, but the Tigers had found a weapon.

* * *

LSU was scared. The Tigers knew full well that Tulane, a well-oiled football machine powered by All-America fullback Eddie Price, was more than capable of burying LSU again if the Wave got rolling—and given an opportunity, knew Tulane would.

Tinsley took extraordinary measures to prevent that possibility, starting *during* the game leading up to Tulane, against a "warm-up," Southeastern Louisiana College.

"The week before the Tulane game," Charles Cusimano, a guard on the '49 Tigers and later a member of the school's Board of Supervisors said, "we had a big lead over Southeastern in the third quarter. Gus Tinsley sent the first and second teams outside the stadium, to a field behind the South End, and we scrimmaged while the scrubs finished the game. Ed McKeever and Norm Cooper, Tinsley's chief assistants, came out with us, and we actually began putting in some of the things we planned to use against Tulane. Can you imagine doing this today?"

Cusimano and Konz agree that McKeever, a longtime associate of Notre Dame's silver-tongued Frank Leahy, motivated the team in the days leading up to Tulane. "During the week," Cusimano said, "he talked to us in groups. Real emotional talks. Before the game, it was right out of Knute Rockne. He started out softly, then built up. At the end, he was screaming."

Konz remembers the spellbinding pregame oratory just before the kickoff, given with tears in McKeever's eyes, of a baby he said died in his arms and how she'd be looking down, watching the game and pulling for the Tigers.

"The most amazing thing of that day," Konz said, "was that nobody was hurt as we all hit the door trying to get out on that field."

* * *

Things started out like a confirmation of Tinsley's worst fears: on the game's first play, going around right end, Eddie Price picked up 20 yards before being knocked out of bounds by Konz. Then Price hit left tackle and gained 15 yards. In two plays the Green Wave was already on LSU's side of the field. Then, in succession, Tulane jumped offside, lost a yard rushing, gained two, and lost six, bringing on a punt—the game's turning point. Konz took the ball on the run at the LSU 8, and, running out of the south end, where the prediction had been painted, headed upfield along the east sideline.

"There was no one around me," Konz said. "I didn't see a single Tulane man on his feet. I just turned a little to the right and made my way downfield. Everyone near me was knocked down. Fact is, some of our guys blocked two men."

It was the opening salvo and seemed to shock the Green Wave, which became erratic offensively. The touchdown held up for a half, and in the third quarter, Tulane pulled itself together for its last major threat, driving to the Tiger 12. LSU's defense asserted itself at that point, throwing the Wave back to the 23 in the next four plays.The Tigers extended their lead when Lee Hedges broke loose on a long run.

Tulane sputtered badly all day, completing only 5-of-14 passes— with LSU picking off an astounding five passes, with Konz getting a school-record three, the last one spurring the Tigers to their final touchdown.

The improbable 21-0 prognostication had come true, representing a 67-point switch from 1948—and Konz, who racked up 173 yards in all-purpose yardage, was the fuse that set it off.

"No team I've ever seen played was close to 100 percent of its capability as this 1949 bunch did against Tulane," Tinsley said afterward, and still insisted decades later. "On every tackle, it seemed like we had four men or more around the ball. Konz played the greatest game at safety I ever witnessed."

* * *

Konz went on from there to a memorable football career. He was All-SEC as a senior, receiving that glowing description from the AP. The MVP of the Blue-Grey Game, Konz was drafted No. 1 by the Cleveland Browns, though he had to put off pro ball for two seasons while he served in the Air Force.

In a career in which he played for three NFL championship and four divisional-title teams, Konz led or tied for the Browns lead in interceptions five of his seven seasons, and retired with a career total of 30. He averaged nearly 40 yards per punt the one season Konz performed that duty, and led the NFL in punt returns with a 14.4 yards per attempt in 1956—one of three years he was selected to the Pro Bowl.

After that season, Konz, who originally signed for $7,500 a year and eventually got to a high of $25,000, went to see Coach Paul Brown about his contract, hoping for a raise. "You know, Coach Brown," Konz said, "I led the NFL in punt returns."

"Paul Brown raised an eyebrow and said sternly to me," Konz recalled, "'What do you think I pay you for?'"

Konz sheepishly signed, and Brown obviously got his money's worth.

Although he graduated with a degree in geology, when Konz' playing days were over he went into sports marketing with famed agent Mark McCormick, and then his own collection agency. Now retired, Konz looks back on a fulfilling career—which almost always centers on the 1949 Tulane-LSU game.

With a wry grin, he said, "That's the one I remember most."

* * *

The '49 Tulane game had far-reaching repercussions for others, for both programs, really, as it ushered in an age of complete dominance in the LSU-Green Wave series. It would be 25 years before the Green Wave would beat the Tigers again.

With some 11th-hour maneuvering the night of the upset, the SEC rescinded its bowl restrictions and—to the Tigers' ultimate regret—LSU got the Sugar Bowl invitation. They were paired with No. 2-ranked Oklahoma.

While Tulane stayed home on January 1, the clock struck midnight for Cinderella, 35-0.

147

CHAPTER 20

DUANE LEOPARD

LSU 7 - Clemson 0
January 1, 1959 • New Orleans, Louisiana

A flash of leather caught Duane Leopard's eye, and he dove for it.

Clemson was putting up a tough fight against No.1-ranked LSU. In the third quarter of the game, the score was still 0-0. It would take a fumble to change that. Clemson tried to punt the ball, but some soggy blades of turf were caught in the center's hand. The snap bounced back on the ground, toward the kicker at the Clemson 11, where Duane Leopard, a defensive lineman for LSU, pounced on the pigskin.

"The [Clemson] guy had the ball, but when he rolled over it, it kind of hung out there, and I went for it," Leopard said.

Three plays later, Billy Cannon fired a nine-yard halfback pass to end Mickey Mangham for the only score of the afternoon. LSU was now in a position to win the football game, but Clemson still had some fight left.

* * *

No matter what happened on New Year's Day, 1959, that particular LSU squad would always be remembered as outstanding. However, their win, coupled with colorful names like "Cannon" and "Chinese Bandits" to go with the team's exploits, assured them a place on the list of legends at LSU. When the season was over, the Tigers were proclaimed the Associated Press' Team of the Year—ahead of the NFL's Baltimore Colts, baseball's New York Yankees, and the NBA's St. Louis Hawks.

Frank Howard, the wily Clemson coach, bought none of the hype—in fact, it all irritated him. He was irked that his 10th-ranked team was a second choice by fans who favored the LSU matchup with Southern Methodist and its spectacular quarterback Don Meredith; and that Clemson (8-2 and the Atlantic Coast Conference champion) was a two-touchdown underdog to the much lighter Bayou Bengals. However, the suggestion that his team might have problems with LSU's backup players aggravated him most.

"The fans can think what they want," Howard snapped. "My boys play like a bunch of one-armed bandits."

Howard was confident that Clemson would blow holes in the smaller LSU line, and that no third-string team, like the Chinese Bandits, could stop his offense. Howard snarled to newsmen, "You can tell them for me that they're gonna have to be No. 1 to beat us. ... That's the way our boys feel about this game."

* * *

When assistant Charlie McClendon offered Leopard the chance to play at LSU, he jumped at the opportunity.

"I don't know if any other school was interested in me or not," he said, "but I'm from Baton Rouge; once I got an offer from LSU I wasn't interested in going anywhere else."

Leopard was part of the recruiting class of 1956. They were undefeated as freshmen, and now at the Sugar Bowl, Leopard, a 6-foot-3, 196-pound junior tackle, was part of another team on its way to an untainted record. However, things were not as Leopard had imagined them.

"When they told me they wanted me to play with the Chinese Bandits," he said, "I didn't want to. I wanted to play with the White Team, the best LSU had."

Regardless which string he played for, Leopard still managed to find his way into Tiger history.

"The Great Wall of China," including Duane Leopard, was too much for Clemson to breach.

* * *

If ever there was an instance of necessity being the mother of football invention, the Chinese Bandits were it. LSU coach Paul Dietzel only had 15 lettermen and three seniors returning from the 1957 Tigers—a team that lost four of its last five games. He had to find a way around the rules so that he could squeeze as much out of his team as possible. During that era, many teams used two platoons, both of which played on offense and defense. It was designed so the second string could keep the starters as fresh as possible. However, the substitution rules were changed before the '58 season. The new rules stipulated that if a player was in a game at the start of a quarter, he could be replaced and then return, but only once in a given period. It was a detrimental change for Dietzel, who had quality front-line athletes but questionable depth.

Dietzel's solution was to divide his squad into three units: the White Team, which was comprised of the best athletes who could play both ways; the Go Team, offensive specialists; and the Chinese Bandits, defensive specialists. The White Team—named after the jerseys worn in practice—would start and play for approximately half of each quarter. The remaining time in the quarter would be divided between the Go Team and the Chinese Bandits.

Contrary to legend, the Bandits were never considered a "third team." LSU's second-best linemen and third-string backs were on the defensive team, while the Go Team was comprised of third-string linemen and second-string backs. This meant that the units were fairly even. However, the Chinese Bandits had a modicum of basic offensive plays they were able to run when caught in a substitution dilemma. They even scored the go-ahead touchdown against Duke on a short drive after blocking a punt. The Go Team, Dietzel admits now, was virtually helpless on defense. Besides, as LSU's sports information director in 1958, Bud Johnson, said, "No unit with a Mel Branch could ever be considered a third team." Leopard wholeheartedly agreed.

Branch, an end, was one of Dietzel's finest linemen—a sterling athlete. However, he had the defensive mentality of a charger, limiting him on offense. Right off, Branch was a quality commodity for the defensive specialists. Gus Kinchen was another stellar defensive player. Unfortunately, he injured his knee in 1956, and many people thought that his career was over. Kinchen spent the next year working for his grant-in-aid as a team manager, and was ready to return to football by '58.

* * *

Unlike the White Team and the Go Team, who were named after their practice jerseys (the Go Team used to be called Gold Team at first, until a sportswriter confused the terms), the defensive team's name came from more colorful origins.

"I got the idea for the Bandits in 1950 when I was a defensive coach under Sid Gillman at the University of Cincinnati," Dietzel recalled. At the time, his favorite cartoon strip was "Terry and the Pirates"—a military adventure set in the Orient. In one particular strip, the leader of the Asian outlaws, Chopsticks Joe, says, "Chinese Bandits are the most vicious people on earth."

The quote struck the young coach. "So I took the cartoon and hung it in the dressing room," Dietzel said. "Our defensive unit [at Cincinnati] became known as the Chinese Bandits. But we were never big winners at Cincinnati, and nobody paid much attention to the Chinese Bandits then." No one paid much attention to the team at LSU in the first 1958 season game against Rice either. In fact, the press only mentioned it in passing as the "reserve platoon." LSU football history would change dramatically when Dietzel took out his first string and replaced it with the largely inexperienced cluster of reserves against Alabama.

"I tell you, it took guts to try it the first time in game conditions," said Charlie McClendon, then Dietzel's first lieutenant and his eventual successor as head coach. "To take out Billy Cannon and your best players and put in an entire team of reserves!"

Dietzel later said he did it because the jacked-up Crimson Tide seemed certain to score, and he didn't want his elite unit, the White Team, to become discouraged. Kinchen said that none of the athletes felt any pressure to perform. In fact, the only thing out of the ordinary that day was the several thousand spectators milling around the sidelines because a section of Mobile's Ladd Memorial Stadium had collapsed earlier in the game. No one was hurt, but some of those fans got a close-up view of a historical moment in Southern football. Kinchen said, "We just went about our jobs."

In three plays, the pumped-up Crimson Tide gained just one yard, settling for a field goal—a milestone goal-line stand. LSU came back to defeat 'Bama 13-3, and Dietzel praised the stand and the unit. The name "Chinese Bandits" was used publicly for the first time, and it was picked up in the press.

"We were fortunate in 1958 that, the first couple of times we put in the Bandits, they managed to get the ball for us; then the thing started snowballing," McClendon recalled. LSU's success and Dietzel's imagination fed off each other, catching the fancy of the college football world. The Chinese Bandits were well-schooled in gang-tackling, and they exceeded expectations during their limited game time.

"They really performed like a great team," Dietzel said. "On film, you'd see nine gold helmets meeting at the ball carrier. They were brilliant at gang-tackling."

There soon was a Chinese war chant, written by Memphis disc jockey Keith Huddleton, which was played whenever the Bandits took the field—and also throughout all of Louisiana at all times of the day. Frequently, the loudest Saturday night roar at the old mossy arena would be when the P.A. announcer would shout, "Here come the Chinese Bandits!"

The Chinese Bandits were a phenomenon. They became a national item, and the most celebrated reserve unit in the history of college football. When *Life* did a spread on the Bayou Bengals, it didn't do stories on Billy Cannon or Paul Dietzel. The Chinese Bandits were *Life's* focus. The esprit de corps of the group was powerful. Dietzel gave them a subtle mark of distinction, socks with red stripes at the top.

When an injury caused Dietzel to juggle his lineups slightly, guard Tommy Lott was offered a promotion to the White Team. However, Lott answered with an indignant stare, and said, "Okay, but as soon as possible I want to get back to the Bandits."

Dietzel later reflected that being a part of that unit "… became a matter of real pride. They were terrific gang-tacklers, and they had speed." They were also reserves and for a reason, but they had amazing hustle and enthusiasm. Dietzel's association with the Bandits was his self-proclaimed greatest thrill in athletics.

* * *

Clemson wasn't the only thing that LSU battled in the Sugar Bowl. They were also pitted against adversity and apathy. While the South Carolinians were enjoying the pregame hospitality and festivities of New Orleans, the Tigers were living and practicing on their deserted campus 80 miles away. School was out for the holidays, and their only reward for the memorable season was more football preparation with no companionship other than teammates and coaches. The only LSU person to take part in the revelry leading up to the game was Dietzel. He went to the Sugar Bowl dinner at famed Antoine's to accept the AP national championship trophy.

On the damp, overcast morning, the Bengals bussed down to Tulane Stadium to meet Howard's determined Clemson Tigers, who seemed to have a monopoly on the breaks, at least in the early going.

Warren Rabb, LSU's starting All-SEC quarterback, fractured his right hand in the second quarter, leaving Durel Matherne of the Go Team as the Tigers' only suited-up signal-caller.

In the second quarter, LSU drove to the Clemson 1. Red Brodnax crashed into the end zone, but fumbled and Clemson recovered. In the first half, LSU lost three serious scoring opportunities, as well as its quarterback. After intermission, things started to change. Clemson drove to the LSU 30, where a lost fumble ended the threat. It was Leopard's recovery of another fumble later in the quarter that led to the Tigers' touchdown.

Late in the game, Clemson unleashed a strong 60-yard drive late in the game. The big Clemson line had begun to wear on the White Team; they picked up a first down, and then another. At that point, Dietzel made a bold decision. He took out the tired White Team and sent in the Bandits to save the game.

"They were rolling," Leopard recalled of the big and bruising Clemson team he trotted out to meet. "And they seemed bent on scoring."

Howard's South Carolinians picked up two more first downs. The last put them at the LSU 25. Two running plays netted one yard, and two incomplete passes returned that ball to LSU with less than two minutes remaining.

"I don't remember everything about it," said Leopard, a retired coach and teacher, and now a mobile home subdivision director in Colorado. "Obviously, though, we did the job—again."

The Bandits made a believer even of Howard. On four separate occasions, the Chinese Bandits were sent in again against Clemson, who ran 19 plays against them, gaining three first downs and 39 yards— an average of just 2.1 yards per snap.

* * *

**Duane Leopard was an integral part of LSU's
celebrated defensive unit.**

Dietzel's theoretical three-team concept worked perfectly in 1958. Over the course of the season, the White Team averaged 35 minutes a game. The Go Team and Chinese Bandits divided the remaining 25 minutes of game time almost evenly. The backup units kept the front-line troops fresh enough to overrun all 11 opponents.

Throughout the entire season, the Chinese Bandits managed to hold up their end of the deal, plus interest. Every time an opponent ran a play against them, they gained less than a yard (0.9).

Photographer Erby Aucoin took a dramatic Sugar Bowl picture that has become an icon of LSU football. Seemingly posed to perfection, the photo shows a Clemson runner vainly tring to scale a pyramid of swarming Chinese Bandits. The photo's title?

"The Great Wall of China."

CHAPTER 21

LEONARD MARSHALL

LSU 20 - Alabama 10
November 6, 1982 • Birmingham, Alabama

Trotting into the tunnel leading to the Legion Field dressing rooms at halftime, Leonard Marshall heard the familiar low growl.

"We've got to do something about that No. 97, slow him down," Paul "Bear" Bryant was saying to one of his assistants. Then, as if the thought just struck him, Bryant added, "If we had him, we might be ahead in this thing."

It gave Marshall—the No. 97 in question—a chill to think he had actually caught the attention of the legendary coach, even though a few years earlier he had turned down a chance to play for Bryant's Crimson Tide.

This, though, was in the heat of battle, not a situation where an assistant saw an athlete, evaluated him, and made a recommendation. That's how the 69-year-old Bryant generally recruited in his latter years. It may not have cost him Marshall, a kid from the Cajun Country-town of Franklin who wanted to go to LSU anyway, but it's interesting to reflect upon: while the Tigers' No. 97 wasn't the only reason for the havoc-wreacking of the Crimson Tide, he was a major cause. Marshall, a defensive tackle, had modest statistics: four tackles and one sack—but another dozen times he either hurried the quarterback or disrupted the play.

Put Marshall in a Crimson Tide jersey and. ... Who knows?

It was a landmark performance because this game—still referred to in Baton Rouge as a 10-point rout—had even the Bear yelling, "Uncle."

The Tigers, leading the nation in defense, held a 'Bama offense that that been averaging 446 yards to 119 ... a Tide offense that had been rushing for 300 yards a game to 45 ... a wishbone system that ran 32 times, and had its ball-carriers caught behind the line 11 times ... a team that had no less than 22 first downs in any of its previous eight games to 6, none in the first half.

That was a watershed moment for LSU, which hadn't beaten Alabama in 11 seasons, and for the SEC. Tiger coach Jerry Stovall became just the sixth SEC coach to best Bryant in a remarkable decade during which Alabama won or shared nine league titles in 11 years. There was no question, though, of which was the better squad on this day. Through the years, LSU had less game domination against some opponents with Tiger scores reaching astronomical proportions.

"I think that's the best beating we've had since the '60s," Bryant said afterward. "LSU had the superior team, and I know they had the best coach. Their defensive line of scrimmage ate our offense. I didn't think anybody could do that."

* * *

This was clearly going to be the SEC game of the year up to that point. Eighth-ranked Alabama and 11th-ranked LSU were first or second in every league statistic.

The Tide, 7-1 going into the game and running the wishbone, was the nation's fourth-best offense. Quarterback Walter Lewis averaged 5.1 yards per carry. When the running game was stifled, Lewis was a 62.4-percent passer, and 'Bama averaged 10 yards per catch.

Prior to the season, Bryant, who coached six national champions, thought this team had the potential to be his best.

"Nothing comes easy in football," Marshall recalled of LSU's preparation. "We knew Alabama was a real load. Remember, though, we

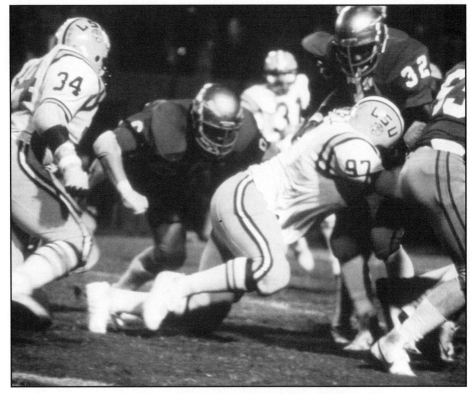

Leonard Marshall (97) stuffs an opposing ball-carrier.

had already beaten Florida [24-13] when the Gators were ranked No. 4. So it wasn't like we hadn't seen a good opponent before. We felt like we could play with anyone."

True enough. The Tigers, 6-0-1, were college football's No. 1 defense, yielding only 193.1 yards per game.

In the second quarter, with Alabama hemmed in by the Tigers' 5-2 defense, LSU scored two touchdowns and a field goal to take a 17-0 lead. It seemed more than enough. At that point, with the Bandit defenders jamming the line, chasing down Tide runners and giving Lewis almost no room to breathe, Alabama had 32 yards of offense—just 10 on the ground. Defensive line coach Pete Jenkins, though, knew it wasn't over. "I told our boys, 'Let's do our celebrating on the way home,'" he said.

Sure enough, 'Bama made a run on the scoreboard, but by the hardest. On its opening second-half possession, 'Bama found a way to move the football, finally picking up first downs—four to be exact—the last at the Tiger 11. Then 'Bama reached the 3, wound up on the 14, and had to settle for a field goal.

On the ensuing kickoff, LSU fumbled, and the Tide recovered on the 28. 'Bama hit a quick pass and had scored 10 points in 25 seconds to make a game of it again.

But LSU allowed 'Bama only two more first downs. For the afternoon, the Tigers forced a total of seven turnovers, including four lost fumbles. Lewis was followed like a fugitive, being brought down trying to run the option a half-dozen times by LSU's linebackers. He mused later, almost unbelievingly, "I have never been caught back there so many times."

On the other side, Tiger quarterback Alan Risher went 20-of-26, and LSU accumulated 321 total yards, almost three times as much as Bama. Coupled with the defense, LSU almost couldn't lose.

Stovall rode the shoulders of his players to the man in the houndstooth check hat, who waited to shake his hand. "He told me," Stovall recalled, "'Congratulations. You deserved to win. Your team played hard.'"

It marked the last time the Bear would tee it up against LSU.

* * *

In his postgame comments, after quipping, "We must have had someone who played well, but I won't know 'till I see the film," Bryant got serious.

"It's been obvious to me the last three or four weeks our team has been poorly prepared," Bryant said. "I ought to be the leader of the Alabama alumni athletic people, alerting the president that we need to make some changes, and we need to start at the top. We need to take inventory of what's going on and do something about it."

Bryant, of course, over the years had perfected the art of poor-mouthing and blame-taking for any deficiencies of his team. This, however, was the first time his public rhetoric along those lines had a serious ring.

Southern sidelines vacant of Bryant were hard to imagine. He was the measuring stick of college football coaches. "If you had to make a living beating Bear Bryant week in and week out, it would be one of the most difficult assignments known to man," Tennessee coach Johnny Majors said. The proof was in the won-loss record. Bryant was an astounding 323-84-17 at four different schools—a victory ratio greater than .750 compiled over five decades—all in dire football straits when the Bear arrived.

Consider these facts:

Charlie McClendon of LSU had a career record of 137-59-7, a .692 winning percentage, but almost a fourth of his defeats came against the Bear, with a 2-14 head-to-head reading.

Doug Dickey, the former Tennessee coach, won three straight from Bryant and two SEC titles before moving to Florida where the Bear frustrated him for nine straight years.

Bill Battle, Dickey's successor at Tennessee, who never had a losing season, won 59-of-83 games for a .723 percentage, and still walked the plank. His record against Bear was 1-6.

Dickey noted, "You're talking about one of the all-time greatest coaches. He didn't get that way by not beating people."

Shortly, Bryant announced his impending retirement from the sidelines, that this would be his last season. Bryant coached the Crimson Tide to a Liberty Bowl victory over Illinois, and a month later he was dead.

* * *

Football wasn't nearly over for Marshall, who went on to an All-Pro career with the New York Giants, playing in two Super Bowls. Now the owner of a financial corporation in Boca Raton, Florida, he also teaches sports management part-time at Seton Hall University. Marshall vividly remembers the day LSU finally bagged the Bear.

"The coaches had us superbly prepared, and the players executed, almost flawlessly," he said. "Coach Bryant was a great coach, and his teams were outstanding. It's what made that '82 game so special."

Leonard Marshall helped disrupt 'Bama's offense.

CHAPTER 22

MATT MAUCK

LSU 31 - Tennessee 20
December 8, 2001 • Atlanta, Georgia

"Who was that masked man?"

The best line on the sports pages of America on December 9, 2001, was penned by Peter Finney of the *New Orleans Times-Picayune* in reference to the SEC Championship game played the previous night. Unheralded—unknown, really—Matt Mauck, a 22-year-old redshirt freshman playing his third game of the season, had come off the bench to quarterback LSU to an upset victory. Running for two touchdowns, he guided the Tigers to a late and crucial time-draining drive that broke Tennessee's spirit.

Mauck's most vivid memory of that night was leaning in the huddle just yards from the Georgia Dome goal posts, looking at the clock winding down and exhorting his teammates: "C'mon, guys, we can close this thing out right here!" They heeded their quarterback, with whom they were just becoming acquainted in the big-game sense, slamming the door shut.

Entering the game, Mauck's season statistics summed just 13 completions in 26 attempts for 157 yards, zero touchdowns, two interceptions. He'd rushed for 30 yards. He left the game, though, as an LSU hero—one with bigger and better things ahead.

"I don't remember that much about it," Mauck said. "I was probably a little nervous at first, but I just did what we prepared for. Things worked out."

On the ensuing play, fourth-and-goal at the Tennessee 1, Mauck handed off to Domanick Davis, who sliced into the end zone to give LSU a 31-20 cushion with 2:26 to play in the Southeastern Conference Championship Game.

With Mauck deftly picking away at the Volunteers defense, the Tigers strung together a 13-play drive that covered 65 yards. As important as the touchdown was the 6:04 the Tigers drained off the clock, precious minutes in which the dangerous Tennessee offense was kept off the field.

Due in no small measure to Mauck, the Tigers, ranked No. 21, had picked themselves off the canvas to KO the second-ranked Volunteers (10-1), a team that needed only a victory over LSU (8-3) to punch a ticket for the BCS title game in the Rose Bowl against Miami.

In typical LSU fashion, the Tigers did things the hard way. In beating the touchdown-favorite Vols, the Bayou Bengals prevailed with what was essentially a second-string backfield. Starting quarterback Rohan Davey, who'd come off the bench a year earlier to spark a second-half rally that in the Peach Bowl on the same field, was knocked out of this one—twice—in the first half with injured ribs. Also in the first 30 minutes, All-SEC running back LaBrandon Toefield injured his left knee, sending him to the sidelines for the rest of the night. Any moving of the ball for LSU would have to be done by backups Mauck and Domanick Davis.

"I had no time to really think about it," Mauck said. "Rohan went down, and I went in. [Perhaps] if I had time to think about the situation, I might have been rattled. But I just went in and did what we had prepared to do."

* * *

Mauck didn't know it, and neither did any member of either of the title-game rosters, but this was going to be payback of sorts of a long-due debt for LSU. In 1959, one week after Billy Cannon's famed punt return

Matt Mauck led the SEC in passing efficiency in 2003.

against Ole Miss, the No. 1-ranked Tigers invaded Knoxville to play an average Tennessee team that would lose four games.

LSU outgained Tennessee 334 yards to 112, but lost two fumbles and had an interception returned for a touchdown—the first trip into the Tiger end zone in 40 quarters. When LSU converted a blocked punt into a touchdown, cutting the Tennessee margin to 14-13 early in the fourth quarter, Paul Dietzel decided to go for two points.

Cannon carried on a power play to the right and seemed to dent the plane of the goal line. The officials ruled he didn't.

To this day, Cannon says, "I'll go to my grave believing I was in."

Even Tennessee hero Johnny Majors, then a Vol assistant and later UT's head coach, shook his head and said, "I'm not saying," when asked years later about Cannon's carry, though he added that, to that point, LSU was the best team ever to play on Shields-Watkins Field.

Now, 42 years later, LSU had the Vols in a similar situation, catching them with visions of No. 1 pennants dancing in their heads.

* * *

LSU had to go much further than the mere 500 miles between Baton Rouge and Atlanta to get to the SEC Championship Game. In their last two years under Coach Gerry DiNardo, the Tigers lost eight games they either led or were in position to win in the fourth quarter—an indication the talent level was higher than LSU's cumulative won-loss record (7-15, 3-13) in 1998-99. That, of course, brought in Nick Saban to straighten out the football program, and he did. The Tigers went to the Peach Bowl in 2000, and they were the preseason favorite to represent the SEC West in the 2001 title game—and here they were, but it took some doing.

After a couple of early victories, LSU's SEC opener with Auburn was postponed because of the 9/11 terrorist attacks. When the schedule resumed on September 29, the Tigers lost 26-18 to Tennessee in Knoxville. That was followed by a 44-15 belting by Florida, and the worst was yet to come. Expected wins against Kentucky and Mississippi State ensued, but the bottom dropped out in a 38-24 meltdown against

Ole Miss—a game in which LSU turnovers accounted for 28 Rebel points.

The Bayou Bengals, thought to be hotshots seven weeks before, were a mediocre 4-3 overall, 2-3 in the conference, and everyone, especially their fans, took every opportunity to remind them of their shortcomings. The sports pages, sports talk shows, and the fans in the street were all counting LSU out. The Tigers began circling the wagons. Linebacker Trev Faulk started scribbling "US 11" on his taped wrists, summing up the team's new us-against-the-world attitude.

Something kicked in. Davey threw for 528 yards in a 35-21 victory at Alabama. Three more opponents, including Auburn in the postponed game, fell in easy fashion.

All of a sudden, and as was predicted in the summer, LSU was the Western Division champ and in the SEC Championship Game. Could the Tigers compete with the mighty Vols? Not according to the pundits and prognosticators across the South, almost all of whom made it seem as if LSU was in over its collective head. Even Vols coach Phil Fulmer, a gentleman who never put up with trash talk or taunting by his squad, wore a rose in his lapel as Tennessee boarded its plane to Atlanta.

One thing was lost in LSU's early loss to the Vols, though. Late in the fourth quarter, LSU had a serious drive going that could have tied the game, perhaps putting the Tigers in position to win in overtime.

LSU had two abstract factors going for it: the Volunteers could be looking past LSU after beating Florida to jump to No. 2 the previous week; and the revived Tigers, on a run that looked impossible a month earlier, knew, even if no one else realized it yet, that they were Tennessee's equal.

As Mauck recalled, "We weren't going just to show up. We knew we'd have to play a good game, but we also knew if we did that we could win."

* * *

Mauck also took a circuitous route to the SEC Championship Game. At Jasper (Indiana) High, he was part of two baseball state championship teams and made the football state championship game his junior season, but lost. By every account, Mauck was a special player at Jasper, one with unusual responsibilities, according to Kurt Gutgsell, the sports director at a Jasper radio station and at a UPN television station, WJTS, that televised every football, basketball and baseball game Mauck played in high school.

Playing in an I-formation system, Mauck would carry 30-35 times a game. Gutgsell pointed out that the Jasper football coach, a coach of more than four decades, saw Mauck as an extension of the coaching staff.

"Matt may have been the first and only quarterback to have the okay to change a play at the line of scrimmage," Gutgsell said. "He would just read the defense and call the play the opposite way."

Mauck originally signed with Saban to play at Michigan State in 1998, but then opted for pro baseball, signing a minor-league contract with the Chicago Cubs. After three years of riding buses along the byways of the Midwest, playing third base and catcher, and realizing he was never going to catch up with upper-classification pro pitching while watching a lot of buddies get cut, college life suddenly began looking better to Mauck.

During downtime, he spent a lot of time talking with friend and roommate Chris Dorsett, a Rutgers grad. Dorsett ended up being cut, but his education led him to becoming an investment banker in Manhattan.

"I had finished college; so no matter what happened in baseball, I could always fall back and get a real job," Dorsett said. "He looked up to that."

Mauck contacted Saban, now at LSU, about the possibility of still playing football. It was a bargain Saban couldn't refuse, getting what the coach knew was a solid prospect—and at no risk. Mauck's contract with the Cubs called for them to pay two years of college costs, so LSU wouldn't have to relinquish a scholarship.

Rohan Davey was firmly entrenched at quarterback after a battle royale for the position the last few years. In recent seasons, LSU had three talented QBs, Josh Booty, Craig Nall, and Davey—all of whom would play in the NFL but none of whom as a starter would satisfy Tiger fans. Booty, the coaches' All-SEC quarterback in 1999, went to the NFL; Nall transferred; and Davey took over at LSU in 2000. That season

Mauck worked the rust off his game as a redshirt under the watchful gaze of offensive coordinator Jimbo Fisher.

Davey had firm control at quarterback in 2001 without a serious challenge to his position, passing for 3,263 yards as the Tigers made their way to the title game. Mauck wasn't even a blip on the LSU radar screen. No one, of course, could have known it at the time, but the SEC Championship Game was just the kind of stage on which Gutgsell said Mauck always excelled.

"Matt was at his best in the big games," the Indiana sports director said. "He could really run the football in open space."

* * *

Things were set into motion with just four minutes gone in the game when, with LSU on the move, Davey took a shot in the ribs from Vols linebacker Keyon Whiteside and was sent to the locker room for x-rays. Mauck grabbed his helmet and raced onto the field while Fisher started adjusting his offensive blueprints. Not nearly the passer that Davey was—as attested by four overthrown passes in his first drive—Mauck was far more mobile. Fisher utilized more QB draws, eventually giving the Vols another runner to think about and defend.

In eight plays—none of which were completed passes but made up for by Tennessee penalties—Mauck slipped through the line four yards for the first points of the night.

The moment had been seized. LSU knew it could move on the vaunted Vols defense.

Tennessee came back, taking a 17-7 lead after Saban made what he later said was "the worst decision of my coaching career," going for it on fourth-and-inches at the Tiger 22.

When LSU didn't make it, the Tigers still kept Tennessee out of the end zone, forcing the Vols to kick a 51-yard field goal, longest in the short history of the championship game. Saban's decision may have been a positive, though, because the players said later it showed the faith he had in them and that they appreciated it.

In the second half, with Davey and Toefield now out for the remainder of the game, Mauck guided the Tigers to 14 unanswered

Matt Mauck was at his best in big games.

points—two field goals by John Corbello and another touchdown by Mauck, this one for 13 yards, and a two-point conversion pass to Josh Reed.

A 21-yard field goal by Tennessee with 9:55 to go had the Vols within hailing distance at 24-20. Mauck took the air out of their sails, though, with the long final drive that ate up most of the clock that put Tennessee behind by more than one possession.

The backups were extraordinary. Mauck, the game's MVP, wasn't spectacular but was efficient with 43 rushing yards—on five seemingly indefensible QB draws—and two touchdowns, and was 5-of-16 for 67 yards. On 16 carries, Davis gained 78 yards and scored the last touchdown that broke Tennessee's back.

The resilient Tiger defense held Travis Stephens—who had run wild the week before against Florida for 226 yards—to 37.

Those performances coalesced to give LSU its first SEC title in 13 years. They went on to defeat Illinois in the Sugar Bowl to complete an improbable six-victory run (three over ranked opponents) and lifted them to a final No. 7 ranking.

* * *

There was more to come for Mauck, whose mobility was restricted after an injury the following season; he became much more of a pocket passer. In 2003, Mauck led the SEC in passing efficiency and quarterbacked LSU to the BCS national championship. Interestingly, Mauck said he probably played better in his LSU coming-out party against Tennessee than he did against Oklahoma in the game for No. 1.

Mauck took his 18-2 record as a starter—a .900 victory ratio that stands as the best in Tiger history—and left LSU football a year early to go to dental school. However, the Denver Broncos drafted him, and Mauck made the team. After thoughts of the Tennessee upset flooded his memory bank, he said, "Now there's a fun game to look back on."

He was unmasked that night, and LSU repaid a long-simmering debt.

CHAPTER 23

FRED
MILLER

LSU 13 - Texas 0
January 1, 1963 • Dallas, Texas

They hit like two rams butting heads.

On the first play from scrimmage, Texas' Ernie Koy took a handoff and was immediately blasted out of the backfield by Tiger tackle Fred Miller. According to McClendon, the six-yard loss, in which the Longhorn ball carrier seemed to be caught under a one-man avalanche, "kind of set the tone for the rest of the day."

In this odd Cotton Bowl pairing, in which the seventh-ranked Tigers were a two-point favorite over the fourth-ranked Longhorns, Texas would never get closer to the LSU goal than the 25-yard line. In other words, they never seriously threatened to score. If ever there was a game of immovable objects, this was it. It turned out that LSU, with a defense featuring All-Americans Miller and safety Jerry Stovall, was more dent-proof than Texas'. In Texas' 9-0-1 season, the Longhorns surrendered a total of 59 points; while LSU, in its first season under McClendon, led the nation in scoring defense, yielding 34 points in their 8-1-1 season.

In a match between two superior football teams, the only real difference between them may have been emotional, founded on a

Fred Miller set the tone against unbeaten Texas in the '63 Cotton Bowl.

perceived affront to the visiting Tigers. Miller said the Tigers felt like an afterthought in the run-up to the Cotton Bowl. According to him, the famed Lone Star State-centric attitude of nothing worthwhile existing outside its borders, hit the Tigers full force.

"We felt slighted in Dallas," Miller recalled. "The press, at the functions, almost everything, it was Texas, Texas, Texas. It was almost as if we were there just so the Cotton Bowl could fill out its ballgame."

* * *

The fact that Miller was even in Dallas may have been the biggest upset of that New Year's Day. LSU was pretty low on his list after having played at Homer High School in the pinecone hills of north Louisiana. Miller was an All-State lineman on a team that never had enough players for a full intra-squad scrimmage. Despite being a team that never dressed out more than 20 players, the "Iron Man" Pelicans reached the Class AA finals.

"I don't know of another high school team that ever captured the public's imagination the way that group of kids did," Glenn Gossett, Homer's first-year coach in 1957, said decades afterward. Miller was a major part of that unexpected success.

"Fred David was a quiet kid who took care of business in a very efficient manner," said Donald Johnson, a Homer assistant at the time. "He developed a reverse spin move to get outside blockers on end sweeps that was not the technique we were teaching at the time, but we didn't correct him because he had the physical ability to make it work."

This is how good the Pelicans were that season: 12 of them received football scholarships—four to LSU.

At first, Miller was not one of the Tiger signees. He had not been enamored with LSU coach Paul Dietzel and originally had signed with Tulane. "I thought the world of [Green Wave coach] Andy Pilney," Miller said, "and I wanted to play for him." The influence of Homer principal Hugh Whatley, a Tulane athlete from 1928-30 and instrumental in the Greenies' 12-7 victory over LSU in his last game, didn't hurt either. However, at the time Miller was searching for his collegiate home, Tulane had extremely stringent standards and, through no fault of his own, Miller didn't meet them. He had only three English credits, all that Homer High offered, and Tulane required four. Miller decided on Texas A&M next. Teammate Ray Wilkins was also headed there. Aggie coach Bear Bryant, though, left for a position at Alabama, leaving that option up in the air.

Dietzel never stopped working his charm on the Miller family, and he managed to convince Miller's mother and sisters that he should play at LSU. The circumstances put Miller in purple-and-gold togs. Wilkins also ended up at LSU. Miller, though never did warm up to Dietzel.

"At least one time I was on the verge of leaving because of him," Miller said. "Charlie Mac talked me out of it, telling me 'From now on I'm your coach.' And he was. I really loved the man. When Coach Mac passed away I grieved like I did for my daddy."

McClendon was the reason Miller was even on the field New Year's Day, 1963. Miller, 6-foot-3, 230-pounds, was redshirted as a sophomore then spent his first two varsity seasons on the Chinese Bandits, and those were very productive years. The Baltimore Colts made Miller a seventh-round future pick after his junior year, and he could have skipped his final year to head for the pros. He returned to LSU mainly because of McClendon. Miller was a force on McClendon's formidable defense, before and during the '63 Cotton Bowl.

"I wanted to play my last year under Coach Mac," Miller said. "He's one of the greatest human beings I've ever been around. ''

* * *

Texas, which put together its first undefeated regular season since 1923, was by far the fastest opponent the Tigers had played. The LSU coaching staff put in a couple of new plays designed to make the Longhorns' speed work to the Tigers' advantage. One play looked like a sweep to one side but wound up as an off-tackle play on the other side; the other had the opening appearance of a quarterback sprint-out which turned out to be a pass to an end cutting across the middle.

"They were our bread and butter," sighed Go Team quarterback Lynn Amedee, who turned out to be LSU's biggest offensive weapon in its convincing victory. "Everytime we needed something, we got it from those plays."

Miller and the Tigers kept Texas at bay throughout the opening 30 minutes. With time trickling away in the first half, and LSU playing a third-and-four at the Texas 34, Amedee sprinted to his right, stopped, and speared tight end Billy Truax for a 22-yard gain. Two plays later, with eight seconds remaining until intermission, Amedee somehow pushed a field goal through the goal posts. A Longhorn got the tip of a finger on the ball and it went over the crossbar in a circular motion instead of end over end.

Amedee kicked off to open the second half, and when Texas' Jerry Cook was hit at the 'Horns' 35 he fumbled. The ball bounced to Amedee at the 37. White Team quarterback Jimmy Field worked the Tigers to the 22, then on a bootleg play, raced for the game's only touchdown. With 29 minutes remaining, LSU concentrated on keeping Texas from hitting a big play. The Tigers were successful, and Amedee kicked a 37-yard field goal in the fourth quarter.

"I never thought the ball would make the crossbar," he said. "There was a little breeze blowing in from the end zone. ...I don't believe I cleared it by more than two feet."

The Tiger defense blunted a couple of drives, including one of the Longhorns' best. Texas drove to the LSU 25, its deepest penetration of the day, which ended with a missed field goal. The 'Horns' also got down to the 30 late in the game, but Stovall intercepted and LSU kept possession to game's end. Accolades were heaped on the Tigers for their masterful defensive performance.

"It's the best team I ever played against in three varsity seasons," Texas All-America linebacker Pat Culpepper said. Longhorn coach Darrell Royal said simply, "We were beaten by a great football team."

Royal, of course, knew what he was talking about. The next season, the Longhorns, composed primarily of the troops who played against LSU, won the national championship.

* * *

Miller went on to an 11-year career in the NFL with the Baltimore Colts whom he played for in three Pro Bowls. Later, he became the vice-president of Ward Machinery. He and wife, Charlene, raised four boys on a 45-acre farm near Charm City, where he experienced the ultimate highs and lows of the game. Miller was a starter in Super Bowl III, in which Joe Namath guaranteed a victory for the 18-point underdog, then backed it up with a 16-7 upset. Miller was captain of the Colts in Super Bowl V, when the Colts beat the Cowboys 16-13 on Jim O'Brien's field goal in the final seconds.

"Not too many people seem to remember we beat the Cowboys, but everybody seems to remember Namath and the Jets beating us," Miller said in exasperation.

He doesn't have the same exasperation in remembering LSU's performance in the '63 Cotton Bowl. Thinking back on what he took as high-hat treatment by Dallas, Miller described it as "one of the most satisfying wins I was ever a part of."

CHAPTER 24

DOUG MOREAU

LSU 13 - Syracuse 10
January 1, 1965 • New Orleans, Louisiana

Doug Moreau mentally lined up the goal posts, 28 yards away, in his crosshairs; then he took several steps backward.

The Tigers calling on Moreau to pull their chestnuts out of the fire was a familiar scene in the fading minutes of LSU football games during the 1964 season. In this particular case, it was against Eastern powerhouse Syracuse in a historically significant game. The 1965 Sugar Bowl was the first since the U.S. Supreme Court had overturned Louisiana laws that prohibited sporting events between black and white athletes. Orangemen running backs Floyd Little and Jim Nance were the first African-Americans to appear on Sugar Bowl rosters since Bobby Grier of Pittsburgh in 1956. They were national figures, having scored a total of 25 touchdowns between them—14 more than LSU had scored as a team in that era when defenses dominated the sport. However, Moreau was the central figure of the game that day, just as he had been for LSU's season as a whole.

Here he was, with 3:48 to play, with victory, defeat, or most likely a frustrating tie, depending on his left-footed kicking accuracy.

"I really was pretty relaxed," Moreau recalled of his field goal. "We were in almost exactly that kind of situation all season long. Close games that went down to the wire were kind of our calling card that particular year. This was nothing new."

Still, the Orangemen didn't have to call a timeout to try to "ice" the Tiger kicker. LSU did it for them. "I needed it," Moreau said. "This was like our game against Mississippi State, when I missed one because I was worn out running pass routes. I remembered that and used this one to catch my breath."

* * *

Moreau's presence colored the entire '64 Tiger season. The 6-foot-1, 180-pound junior had been switched from end the previous season in part because of a change in offenses mandated by a rash of injuries. Coach Charlie McClendon went to a flanker formation, putting Moreau farther out on the line in the position now known as "split end," where the Tigers could make better use of his pass-catching and big-play talents. The only problem with this is that, without his blocking, the change diluted LSU's power-running ability. All season, the Tigers could move effectively from 20 to 20, then bog down. Of the 21 times LSU would penetrate the opposition's 10-yard line that season, the Tigers scored only five touchdowns. This forced LSU to turn to a weapon that was an afterthought in those days: the field goal. In the regular season, Moreau kicked 13, which was the NCAA record. The following year Charlie Gogolak of Princeton kicked 16, and from then on, the field goal became an indispensable part of virtually every offense.

Ironically, Moreau, now the district attorney of Baton Rouge and color analyst of Tiger radio broadcasts, never kicked a field goal in his life until he got to LSU. In fact, Doug was a self-taught kicker. A telephone line stretched across the yard of Moreau's Baton Rouge home, and it proved to be the perfect enticement for any kid infatuated with football. "It wasn't a case of looking for something to kick over," he said. "It was just there."

"Kicking wasn't even a big deal when I got to LSU. It wasn't like it is now, with specialists for every phase of the game, punting, place-

Doug Moreau spent 1964 bailing out the Tigers.

Making a juggling catch against Syracuse is flanker Doug Moreau (80).

kicking, third-down players," Moreau said. "They just looked for athletes."

Not many eyes were cast in Moreau's direction. He got one late scholarship offer, from LSU; though weeks later, after Coach Paul Dietzel left for Army, Moreau received an appointment to West Point. Dietzel had seen potential in Moreau's blocking and receiving skills. However, Moreau decided to stick to his commitment to LSU. One of the first things he heard when the freshman team assembled was a coach asking in a shout whether anybody wanted to kick.

"Seven or eight of us put up our hands," Moreau said. "That's just how it was in those days. There just wasn't any high priority on kickers."

Moreau won the job and did a commendable job in 1963 as a sophomore, kicking four field goals. The following season, LSU realized just how lucky they were that (1) Dietzel offered his last scholarship to Moreau, and (2) Doug raised his hand when the call went out for kickers. In the opening game of 1964, Moreau's 34-yard field goal was the clincher in a 9-6 victory over Texas A&M, and against Rice a week later he booted a 28-yarder in the final minutes for a 3-0 LSU win. He kicked one against Tennessee to give LSU a 3-3 standoff (though Moreau remembers even more the two he missed against the Vols). In the then-white hot rivalry with Ole Miss, LSU pulled out an improbable 11-10 victory after the Tigers recovered a fumble, scored a late touchdown, then went for two. Despite the fingertips of a Rebel defender brushing the ball, Moreau made the catch in the end zone with barely an inch to spare before going out of bounds. He also managed to catch two touchdown passes in a 14-10 nail-biter against Mississippi State.

It was no secret that at crunch time, LSU looked to Moreau, who scored 73 of the Bengals' 115 points in the regular season—63 percent of the LSU total. The dramatic Ole Miss victory is the one Tiger fans most often associate with Moreau; however, he ranks the Sugar Bowl just as memorable.

* * *

A sports-minded youngster, Moreau remembers watching the news when Georgia Gov. Marvin Griffin thundered, "The South stands at Armageddon," in opposition to a 1956 Sugar Bowl pairing of Georgia Tech and the University of Pittsburgh, which had a black player. He recalled thinking, "This sounds stupid." The Louisiana legislature did not agree. They enacted more than a dozen segregation laws—one of which prohibited racially mixed athletic events. It should be noted that the Sugar Bowl fought the legislation; but it wasn't until January 8, 1964, when the U.S. Supreme Court overruled the laws, that it was possible for another integrated team to play a postseason game in Louisiana.

The New Orleans media pushed hard for an invitation to Syracuse, the best in the East, with marquee names like Little and Nance—a one-two punch that combined for 1,779 yards and more than two touchdowns a game.

"The East vs. the South competition," wrote columnist Peter Finney, "as far as I'm concerned has more postseason appeal than the SWC vs. SEC or All-SEC matches we've been getting." Buddy Diliberto, another media voice, said later, "For one thing, we thought it would be a dramatic way to end the segregation thing."

It was, but some of the luster was taken off the match when Syracuse lost its final game to West Virginia, dropping the Orange record to 7-3; and LSU lost a hurricane-delayed final game to Florida, with the Tigers' record dipping to 7-2-1.

"Considering everything," Diliberto said later, "it was still the right choice."

The social ramifications weren't a major concern to LSU players. According to Moreau, the issue was never even brought up during pregame preparations. To the Tiger players, it was an exciting pairing.

"You have to remember the times," Moreau said. "This was before ESPN and wall-to-wall games on cable. You were lucky to see a game a week on television. We thought it was going to be fun playing against guys from another part of the country, a team and players we had only read about. Little and Nance had had our complete attention, but because they were great football players, not because of race."

* * *

In a game that would feature all manner of scoring, LSU's first points came when Tiger lineman George Rice wrapped up Little in the end zone for a safety. The Orangemen were stymied offensively, but certainly not defensively. Dennis Reilly blocked an LSU punt, and Bradlee Clarke ran it 28 yards into the end zone to put Syracuse up 10-2. LSU, 5½ point favorites, knew they were in for a battle to the wire.

On the first possession of the second half, at the Tiger 43, substitute LSU quarterback Billy Ezell stepped into the huddle and called "I-26-wide-and-go." The play would send Moreau out as a lone receiver. He would run downfield, fake a cut to the sideline, and then head for the end zone. In the first quarter, Moreau had cleanly beaten defensive back

Will Hunter by 15 yards on the same play, but Ezell overthrew him. This time Ezell pumped once and lofted the ball to Moreau at the 25. Moreau said of the second-and-16 play, "When I broke straight, there was the ball." The touchdown covered 57 yards.

A two-point conversion pulled LSU even at 10. That's where things stood until the game moved into the latter stages of the fourth quarter, when starting quarterback Pat Screen broke off a 23-yard gain on a keeper, putting LSU at the Syracuse 26. The Tigers nudged down to the 8 when McClendon called on Moreau to try to nail his 14th field goal of the season.

"The kick felt good when it left my shoe," Moreau said of the 28-yard field goal, "then, before I looked up, Billy [Ezell, the holder] screamed, 'It's good!'"

In a game eerily similar to LSU's season as an entity, Moreau was not only was responsible for the winning play, in addition, he had scored nine of the Tigers' 13 points. An uncle who lived in New York sent Doug a newspaper account of the game featuring his game-winning heroics.

"Again, remember, this was long before the internet and relatively easy access to newspapers almost anywhere," Moreau said. "So when I opened it up and read about our team winning the Sugar Bowl, it was also the first time in my life I ever read *The New York Times*."

CHAPTER 25

JOSH REED

LSU 47 - Illinois 34
January 1, 2002 • New Orleans, Louisiana

After spending hours watching film to prepare for the Sugar Bowl, Brandon Lloyd gave his counterpart, Josh Reed, two thumbs up. A receiver for Big Ten champion Illinois, Lloyd wasn't searching for chinks in the LSU secondary—rather he was looking for tips from his opponent's top receiver.

"I watched tape of Josh Reed before I watched tape of the LSU defense," Lloyd said in reference to LSU's redshirt junior, who would be playing the last game of a spectacular season and, ultimately, his career. "Reed is not that fast, but he runs good routes. I'm more of a receiver-receiver type—I line up out wide about 90 percent of the time. Josh Reed moves everywhere. He's so physical and so strong; he can line up in the slot against linebackers and safeties. He's a good receiver—especially in getting yards after the catch."

The rest of the Fightin' Illini would soon agree.

Soon after the opening kickoff, Reed caught his first pass of the night. Then his second … then his third … and so on. Reed seemed to be everywhere the ball was, and on this night, he racked up 14 receptions for 239 yards—both Sugar Bowl records.

"It was satisfying," Reed recalled. "Everyone was saying how talented they were in the secondary, so we had a challenge."

The Illinois defensive perimeter, anchored by cornerback Eugene Wilson (six interceptions), was a major factor in its 10-1 regular season. This matchup pitted strength versus strength. LSU boasted a dazzling offensive unit that featured the pitch-and-catch combination of quarterback Rohan Davey and Reed.

At 5 feet, 11 inches, 198 pounds, Reed was considered slower and shorter than any of the Tiger pass-catchers, but he still received the Biletnikoff Award—given to college football's outstanding receiver, after setting LSU and SEC season records in yards receiving (1,740), receptions (94), and games with at least 100 yards receiving (10).

"He was just amazing," Davey said. "Josh always found a way to get open. I'd go through my progressions, and he might be covered. I'd go to my second, then third options, and then back to Josh. By that time, he would be open."

Reed spent most of the evening against Illinois that way—open.

* * *

Reed took a roundabout route to the Biletnikoff Award, beginning as a promising backfield prospect. "Promising," however, was about the most hopeful word he heard about his playing potential.

"I came to LSU as a tailback," Reed, who grew up in Rayne, Louisiana (where he rushed for more than 2,000 yards in both his junior and senior seasons). "We were pretty stacked there with LeBrandon Toefield, Rondell Mealy, and Domanick Davis [all of whom saw duty in the NFL], so I wasn't getting much of a chance at carrying the ball." In 1999, when Reed was a redshirt freshman, he was getting more touches as a kick return specialist than as a tailback. "I really was disappointed, even frustrated," he recalled.

Still, at least one person spotted something ultraspecial in Reed. Tiger quarterback Josh Booty noticed in practice that Reed had a real knack of making defenders miss him on their first attempts, giving the offense added yardage. "Didn't know what kind of hands he had," Booty said. "I just knew what he could do after the catch. It's like giving a running back a head start into the open field."

Booty was convinced Reed should have more of a role on the Tiger team and took it upon himself to mention that to Coach Gerry DiNardo. A flustered Reed also eventually went to the head coach and told him he'd welcome a new position if it meant more playing time. In those dark, final days of the DiNardo regime, anything might be worth trying. By the ninth game of '99, at No. 12 Alabama, his Tigers were 2-6 and on a six-game losing skein; and DiNardo told Reed to get ready—that a few passes might be coming his way.

Unknown at the time, it was the beginning of something big. Alabama prevailed 23-17, but LSU had a shot at the end due to Reed. In the last minutes, Booty drove the Tigers 78 yards to within a yard of the 'Bama end zone, with Reed catching two passes totaling 33 yards. On the game's last play, though, Booty tried to run it in instead of attempting a pass and was stopped inches short.

From then on, though, Reed was an integral part of the LSU offense. When he took over as coach in 2000, one of the first things that struck Nick Saban, was Reed's ability to "… stick a cleat in the ground and turn." Starting sporadically as a sophomore, Reed still had 65 catches for 1,127 yards and 10 touchdowns. In his eye-popping 2001 regular season, though, Reed set LSU and SEC season records for catches and yardage.

* * *

The Tigers were inconsistent in the first half of 2001, winning four games and losing three, including three of their five SEC games. The bottom seemed to fall out when LSU lost to a clearly inferior Ole Miss team, which turned two Tiger turnovers and a blocked punt into 21 points and a 35-24 Rebel victory. The next week, ironically against Alabama—the same team he first faced as a receiver—Reed and Davey made history, linking up 19 times for 293 yards, both LSU and SEC records, and LSU won 35-21. The Tigers seemed to catch fire, averaging 35 points over their final seven games, including the SEC Championship Game and the Sugar Bowl, to finish with a 10-3 record.

Josh Reed looks for the end zone in the Sugar Bowl.

Obviously, Reed, who caught 62 passes over that span, was a major part of that ignition.

Pro scouting reports described him thusly: "The centerpiece of LSU's offensive revival. Finds the open spots on the field to break long gains."

Another read: "LSU has one great WR in Josh Reed, who does not have anything close to blazing speed, but he's a converted RB with tremendous ball skills, great cutting ability and excellent running ability after the catch."

Reed's 2001 production that had football aficionados raving:

Tulane—135 (yards)-6 (receptions)
Utah State—124-5
Tennessee—125-7
Florida—123-6
Kentucky—160-8
Miss. State—146-10
Ole Miss—85-3
Middle Tennessee—120-9
Alabama—293-19
Arkansas –183-7
Auburn—186-10
(SEC championship game) Tennessee—60-4
(Sugar Bowl) Illinois—239-14

"Yeah, he's the best in the country," Davey said simply in trying to explain his battery-mate's uncanny ability to escape close defense. "A normal receiver's separation is two or three yards," Davey said. "Josh Reed's separation is five to seven yards. You could punt the ball in there."

* * *

Three weeks after lighting up Alabama, Reed received the Biletnikoff. In Baton Rouge practicing with his team, he said in a taped clip: "This is really unexpected. I never thought when I lined up against Alabama in the ninth week of the season in 1999 that I would be in this

The 2001 Biletnikoff recipient, Josh Reed.

position in such a short time. I've been very fortunate to always have great teammates and great coaches around me that have made this possible. This has all happened so fast it hasn't really sunk in yet."

Of course, he was fibbing. ...

"If I wasn't going to win, why did they want a clip of me accepting it?" Reed chuckled later.

LSU beat Tennessee to get to the Sugar Bowl to play Illinois—displaced from the Rose Bowl, which was that year's site of the BCS national title game. The Illini had many offensive weapons to be concerned about, but none more dangerous than Reed, who entered the game averaging 145 yards receiving (tops nationally) and 7.83 catches per game (third-best nationally).

Against the Fightin' Illini, he would exceed both.

In the highest-scoring Sugar Bowl ever—one in which tailback Domanick Davis ran for four touchdowns and LSU's offense gained a Sugar Bowl-record 595 yards—Reed was most spectacular with his passel of receptions and yardage, and his two touchdowns (32 and five yards, respectively).

The performance allowed Reed to leave the college game as the first player in SEC history to gain 3,000 yards receiving in a career. He finished with 167 receptions for 3,001 yards (18.0 yards per catch) and 17 touchdowns—starting in just 15 of his 31 games played.

"That Alabama game was certainly special—obviously the most productive game I ever had," Reed admitted. "But the Sugar Bowl was special, too. It allowed me to finish with a bang."

CHAPTER 26

JOHNNY ROBINSON

LSU 62 - Tulane 0
November 22, 1958 • New Orleans, Louisiana

The mood in the locker room was somber as the coaches and players quietly talked over strategy.

"There wasn't panic or anything," Johnny Robinson said. "There was, maybe, a little sense of apprehension because things weren't going the way they were drawn up."

The Tigers were on the verge of their first undefeated, untied season in 50 years—not to mention the national championship—but their archrival Tulane, a football Lilliputian with a 3-6 record, was playing LSU to a standstill with the largest SEC crowd in history, 83,221 people, looking on. This was a very bad time for their plays to misfire.

It was halftime and LSU led 6-0 on a short run by Billy Cannon, but clearly the Green Wave was hanging with the Tigers, awaiting one big break and confirming what some thought.

Looks—and records—can be deceptive. Among Tulane's victims in '58 was Alabama (12-7), and Crimson Tide coach Bear Bryant said afterward: "They're the best defensive team I've seen this season." And Bryant had seen LSU as well, in a 13-3 Tiger victory. Even some of the Tigers were wary of the Green Wave, a seven-point underdog.

"Richie Petitbon and Tommy Mason were on that Tulane team," Robinson said, "and common sense will tell you that athletes like that can beat you with a good game and a couple of breaks." LSU fans, of course, weren't buying into that logic. They were after blood because Tulane halfback Claude "Boo" Mason, Tommy's older brother, had declared, "We'll beat LSU because they'll choke."

Tiger coach Paul Dietzel, a master football psychologist, played up the comment for all it was worth. Not only was Dietzel a coach, but he was also an artist. He decorated the Tiger locker room and training quarters with cartoons, newspaper clippings, diagrams, and paste-ups pertaining to the "choke" quote. He had photo enlargements made of the insulting words, and there was no place in the Tiger team quarters where they wouldn't be seen. There was no possibility of LSU overlooking Tulane. However, after 30 minutes of football, the Green Wave was within a touchdown and extra point of making Boo Mason's prediction come true.

In that era, national championships were determined by what a team did in the regular season, not after the bowls. This was the Tigers' 10th, and last, game of the 1958 regular season. If LSU stubbed its paw, everything the team had accomplished throughout the season would be for naught. Even a close game against Tulane could do in the Tigers. There was a definite Midwest bias in the voting at the time, and Iowa, with a 7-1-1 record, was second in the Associated Press and United Press International polls. The Hawkeyes, whose coach, Forest Evashevski, coincidentally helped Dietzel install LSU's wing-T offense, would finish No. 1 in the Football Writers of America poll; and Notre Dame, with a 6-4 record, would receive first-place votes in the final AP ballot. In any case, the Tigers felt that it might take a big win in order to eliminate the nail-biting while the final votes were counted.

"I wouldn't say we were worried," Robinson said. "I would admit there was sort of an uneasy feeling that we'd better start getting things together—and quickly."

* * *

Johnny Robinson was a first-team All-SEC member.

An early third-quarter interception led to an LSU touchdown, and provided the Tigers with some breathing room. Then, Robinson went 34 yards for a touchdown on an end-around. The rout was on. In the fourth quarter, sandwiched around other Tiger scores, Robinson made a sensational catch and streaked 45 yards for a touchdown. There was another scoring reception of 23 yards, and a returned punt of 47 yards.

In a time when players went both ways, and when a three-touchdown difference was thought of as a rout, LSU scored 56 points in the second half against Tulane. With five touchdowns under their pads, the Tigers stood along the east sideline chanting, "Choke, choke, choke" to their demoralized opponents.

No Tiger had a bad game that day. Cannon finished with three touchdowns and 117 yards rushing, but his teammate Robinson had 91 yards rushing to go with his receiving, return mileage, and four touchdowns. It was enough to garner Robinson "Back of the Week" accolades. LSU was proclaimed No. 1 in a landslide in both principal polls.

"That Tulane game is one I'll always remember," Robinson said, "not just because I had a good day, but because it was the one in which we cemented the national championship."

* * *

Robinson was one of the most versatile athletes ever to play at LSU, although he got only one offer of an athletic grant-in-aid. Dietzel says he wanted Robinson the first time he saw him play, but Johnny suspected he was signed late in the recruiting season because his dad, W.T. "Dub" Robinson, was the Tiger tennis coach.

Robinson played at University High, a small school on the LSU campus where the professors and upper-Baton Rouge elite often sent their kids. There, he was a good football player, a tennis champion, a 30-points-per-game basketball guard, and a .500 hitter on his American Legion team.

Robinson said that he probably could have gotten a tennis scholarship to go to college but that he wanted to play football. In football's offseason he played tennis, winning an SEC singles title in the spring of '58, and teaming with his brother Tommy in winning the SEC doubles championship the next year.

In football, however, he was always the "other halfback," always overshadowed by the presence of Billy Cannon, a two-time All-American and the 1959 Heisman Trophy recipient. It was cliché around Louisiana whenever his name was mentioned to say Robinson would have been an All-American at any other school.

As it was, Robinson was All-SEC, becoming part of one of the most remarkable notes in conference annals. Robinson was one of three Tigers—each from Baton Rouge—to be named to the first-team All-SEC backfield. Quarterback Warren Rabb from Baton Rouge High, and Cannon, from Istrouma High, were the others.

* * *

While LSU fans appreciated Robinson's talents, it wasn't until he got to pro football that he blossomed as a truly great football player. Drafted third by the Detroit Lions, he found himself caught up in the "war" between the National Football League and new American Football League. Robinson opted to play for the AFL's Kansas City Chiefs, where he would help make history.

Robinson excelled as a running back for his first two pro seasons, gaining 658 yards, scoring six touchdowns rushing, and catching 77 passes for 1,228 yards and nine more touchdowns. Despite this, the formidable presence of Abner Haynes gave Chiefs coach Hank Stram some options. Stram asked Robinson to move to defense.

"He was a tremendous offensive player," Stram said, who coached the Chiefs throughout Robinson's career. "Johnny could have been a major pro running back. But we had good backs. We needed defensive players, and Johnny was a good enough athlete to make the shift. He didn't want to at first, but I explained to him this would prolong his career. Johnny ended up playing 12 years and was the premier safety of the 1960s." That's not just one man's opinion. In the NFL's official history, *75 Seasons*, the free safety of that decade is Robinson.

Robinson is a central figure in one of the most memorable Super Bowl photographs; catching the play that iced the Kansas City Chiefs'

Johnny Robinson broke open the '58 Tulane game.

greatest victory, a 23-7 steamrolling of the Minnesota Vikings in 1970. In the picture, Robinson is sprawled on the turf of Tulane Stadium, cradling a football in one arm and holding up one finger as his Chiefs teammates rush to congratulate him.

"Whenever you needed a big play, Johnny was there to make it," K.C. quarterback Lenny Dawson said of Robinson.

That day was a prime example of Robinson's value to his team. Not only did he make the interception that sealed the doom of the Vikings, but he did it with three broken ribs. He was a force in pro football, leading the AFL twice and the NFL once in interceptions, becoming the oldest player to do so in 1971 at 33, and racking up 57 career interceptions, a number still in the top 10 of pro football. Robinson, who was a six-time All-AFL selection, was named to the AFL Hall of Fame as a safety.

"It's really a disgrace he's not in the [Pro Football} Hall of Fame," added Stram, himself enshrined at Canton, Ohio.

* * *

It wasn't until long after Robinson left football that he found his calling, and began the most rewarding phase of his life.

"The Lord works in mysterious ways," Robinson said in wonder when asked of his personal road to his mission in life.

The son of a Baptist deacon who was a staunch pillar of the community, Robinson was magnetized to all the vices his father decried. With dark, matinee-idol looks, Robinson was always a ladies man. And, being the social creature he was, Robinson started drinking, although he said he never did really like the taste of alcohol. He got used to libation, especially in Kansas City, where he owned a nightclub.

Robinson retired from pro football after the '71 season, partly because he was essentially playing for nothing because of a divorce, and partly because of an unrelenting pain in his neck. He got an assistant coaching job with the Jacksonville Sharks of the World Football League. When the WFL folded in 1975, Robinson scouted for the Chiefs, lived on the beach, and boozed it up while trying to decide what his next move would be.

One day, as he headed to a liquor store to buy three quarts of whiskey, Robinson's eye caught a neon sign that said "Our Father's Bookstore." Robinson went inside the shop, and engaged in conversation with the owner, Virginia Dextor. She ended up inviting him to accompany her to the Beaches Chapel Christian Church. It was there that Robinson heard the sermon that "staggered" him.

"I went home in awe that the Lord was real," Robinson said. "I had been churched as a kid, but all I seemed to hear before was doctrine. I didn't realize God was alive and he loved me."

He went home and poured out all of the whiskey in the house. Robinson felt as if he finally had a direction in life. He hasn't had a drink or lit up a cigarette since. Returning to his native state as an assistant football and head tennis coach at Northeast Louisiana University, Robinson began studying for the ministry and began a chaplaincy with the Monroe, Louisiana, police department. "One of the only two jobs you can do without a degree," he joked of his failure to return to LSU and graduate, "preach and paint." Robinson was eventually ordained with the World Ministry Fellowship.

The one complication in Robinson's life was the increasing pain in his neck. He said the diagnosis was a form of rheumatoid arthritis in the spine, which doctors termed incurable. The condition had deteriorated to the point that Robinson needed to walk with a cane. Physicians showed him pictures of hunched-over men whose necks were fused in one position and told him there was a possibility that could be his future.

According to Robinson, when he became associate pastor of a small Monroe Baptist church, he explained his plight to some of the congregation. They took up the cause and began praying for him an hour a day. One morning, after months had gone by, Robinson rolled out of bed. The instant his foot hit the floor, he said, "I knew it was gone. I was healed."

* * *

Robinson's chaplaincy with the Monroe Police Department led him to an ancillary ministry for jail inmates. It was this work that first brought the plight of abused children to his attention. A social worker told Robinson of one boy she was concerned for. He was a 10-year-old incarcerated in the Louisiana Training Institute, a place where incorrigible youth are placed. When Robinson went to see the judge in the case, he was told that the boy was "one of the roughest kids for his age we've ever had."

"When I went out to pick him up," said Robinson, admitting the sight of the child stirred his soul, "I found a kid putting up a tough front, but a scared little boy who had been in trouble all his life, who had been abused by the other kids in the prison, and who told me of experiences

I couldn't imagine any 10-year-old having gone through. I thought about how his life was going to be scarred. I decided I wanted very much to help him, and other kids like him."

Today the sectarian Johnny Robinson Boys Ranch in Monroe is a beehive of activity. Forty-five boys, the maximum number, up to the age of 16, live at the home and are cared for by a staff of 30, including Robinson's wife Wanda, son Matt, eight daycare workers, and three cooks. Teachers tutor students, as well as work with special education pupils.

The ranch is a $1 million-a-year operation, and more than a thousand adolescent boys and young men have passed through its doors. However, putting adolescents on the straight and narrow when they've been sidetracked so early in life isn't easy. Robinson feels a fulfillment with the number of kids he's helped, but admits he hasn't reached them all.

"You know," Robinson said, "I think at first I thought this was going to be something like a Bing Crosby movie. We'd get these kids that needed help, and we'd provide everything they required, including the love and attention they weren't getting at home, and there would always be a happy ending. We discovered life doesn't always work like that, though somebody has to try to help, to give a hand. A good family is so important, someone to put them to bed, someone to make sure they have enough to eat, someone they know cares about them."

Though his is a golden name from their home state and from pro sports, Robinson said it's not a lever in getting to some of his boys. Even with mementos of his exploits displayed in the house, "These kids don't know me or what I did," Robinson said. "For the ones that do, it was so long ago as to be irrelevant. I could bring in Joe Montana or Michael Jordan and not many would be impressed, let alone Johnny Robinson."

It doesn't matter. Despite all of his athletic accomplishments, Robinson seldom talks about them; he would rather discuss the profound gratification he has realized in what he calls his mission in life.

He said, "This is what the Lord has called me to do."

CHAPTER 27

JaMARCUS RUSSELL

LSU 35 - Arizona State 31
September 10, 2005 • Tempe, Arizona

The bedraggled and bone-weary LSU Tigers, freshly evacuated from America's Vale of Tears, had given it their all in the Valley of the Sun. Any long-shot chance of a victory, though, seemed to have blown away in the gales that had flattened their families' homes and forever changed their lives.

The Katrina Season had begun, and the Arizona State Sun Devils had caged the Tigers just enough—needing one more defensive stop in the remaining 73 seconds remaining to cement their 31-28 lead and send LSU packing. Out of field-goal range at the ASU 39, the Tigers faced a fourth-and-10.

The bedeviled Tigers—wearing helmets with fleur-de-lis decals, the symbol of the now flooded and ravaged city of New Orleans, where much of the team called home—committed enough gaffes to lose three games. But they were displaying heart summoned from strife, and they stayed with their worthy opponent most of the way.

Now, though, do or die stared them in the face—and things weren't looking good. Sophomore quarterback JaMarcus Russell rolled right, then, spotting a receiver adlibbing his route, he reversed directions and scampered ahead of the charging Sun Devils linemen. Early Doucet—having dropped three previous passes—seemed clear for an instant. On the sidelines, offensive coordinator Jimbo Fisher started screaming at Russell, "Stick it in there! STICK IT IN THERE!"

But he didn't—he waited briefly before letting it fly.

* * *

In the very disunited state of Louisiana—Catholic and Mediterranean in the south, Protestant and Anglo-Saxon in the north, black versus white, rich versus poor, urban versus rural—Louisiana does have one unifying force: the LSU Tigers.

The late governor John J. McKeithen once stated as much. "[The Bayou Bengals] pump the blood of Louisiana. The spirit of the state flows from them."

No one could seriously equate anything close between mere sports and catastrophic events, but there was a ring of truth about the relationship between Louisiana and its Tigers. "What their Tigers do on the field matters to the people here, carries to their sense of fulfillment or disappointment much more than in other places," McKeithen also reflected. "They are a very real part of our life. When things are going good at LSU, people in the hills of the north to those near the Gulf of Mexico to the south seem to walk with a lighter gait, seem to laugh a lot more, seem to live a lot easier.

"And when things are not going so well, when our people are in dire straits, eventually something the Tigers do will lift us up, give us something that represents hope when it's running low for some folks."

As the state buckled beneath the wrath of twin killer hurricanes, Katrina then Rita, spirit and hope were never lower in Louisiana. Tens of thousands of homes were destroyed by ferocious winds, breached levees and violent flooding, displacing hundreds of thousands of people to faraway places—at least those fortunate ones, those who finally saw sunshine with life and limb intact.

This was the crucible of Louisiana, and the Season of Katrina for the LSU Tigers.

* * *

JaMarcus Russell under center in the Season of Katrina.

No LSU team—maybe no team anywhere—ever had a run-up to a season opener like this one. New coach Les Miles, who brought an almost completely new staff and system, had lost his best running back, Alley Broussard, for the season with a torn ACL suffered in practice. Starters linebacker E.J. Kuale and receiver Dwayne Bowe also had to sit out the first game due to serious, but lesser injuries. The schedule had been radically altered due to Katrina as well. Ranked No. 5 in preseason polls, LSU was supposed to open the season with three straight home games, hosting North Texas, Arizona State, and then Tennessee. Yet, after Katrina made landfall, the North Texas game was postponed; and with LSU's campus functioning as a medical center and refuge for almost 35,000 sick, injured, and dispossessed, the Arizona State game was transplanted to the desert, just five days before its scheduled date.

Blackhawk helicopters provided a surreal daily spectacle as they soared over the LSU practice fields, transporting the injured, sick, and weary for treatment at the Maravich Assembly Center, just across the street from Tiger Stadium, which was being used as a triage unit during the emergency. Asked to take in some of the homeless, the Tigers themselves were suffering from more than a lack of space. Fatigue, lack of sleep, and forced poor eating habits had resulted in a per-player average of seven pounds lost—some twice as much.

Six-foot-five, 250-pound JaMarcus Russell—one of America's most sought-after prospects out of Williamson High School in Mobile, Alabama—opened his two-bedroom apartment to 23 friends and relatives, including rhythm-and-blues legend Fats Domino, grandfather to Russell's girlfriend, Chantel Brimmer. The perpetual stress wore Russell down as it did everyone else, and sleepless nights turned into zombie-like practices the following mornings.

"I figured God put me in a situation to help someone else," Russell reflected. "He'll help me pull through and finish."

* * *

No football team had ever been received by a more gracious host than Arizona State. LSU fight songs bellowed through the stadium speakers, and the end zone was painted to read, "Together We Stand," flanked by each school's colors. Even Sun Devils coach Dirk Koetter purchased tickets for 55 displaced students from—of all places—Tulane, who temporarily had to enroll at ASU.

To give LSU the game, though, was too much to ask of Arizona State, 1-0 and ranked No. 15 entering the game. In fact, the Tiger defense seemed like more of a suggestion than a force to ASU quarterback Sam Keller, who welcomed LSU with four touchdowns and 481 of the Devils' 560 total yards.

To worsen matters, Tiger defenders let two interceptions slip through the their fingers; their receivers combined to drop five passes, including one that seemed a certain touchdown; and a frustrating 11-minute, 19-play drive from the LSU goal line ended at the ASU 6 after Russell fumbled the snap—a miscue that led to Keller's first touchdown pass.

By the fourth quarter, the seemingly down-and-out Tigers were behind 17-7. Then, LSU was energized after blocking two kicks—a field-goal attempt, then a punt—both of which were returned for touchdowns within an 80-second span. After a furious exchange of points that put the Sun Devils back in front 31-28, LSU got what seemed to be its last opportunity, taking over at their own 9-yard line. Looking past the insurmountable task before him, Russell said he never doubted the outcome.

"Look, it was the beginning of a new season and I was the starting quarterback," he recalled. "It was a great feeling. I was never nervous [against Arizona State]. We got the blocked kick and blocked punt for touchdowns; and I felt there was no turning us back, that we would come out with a win."

Guiding the Bengals to Arizona State's 39-yard line, he speared Doucet a couple times, erasing the receiver's earlier mishaps.

"I admit I was frustrated a little," Russell said of his wide-out's earlier drops. "But I looked at it like, 'Stuff happens.' I don't always make perfect throws, so they could blame me just as much. I couldn't really blame them for not catching every pass."

The payoff pass, though, started as a play to orchestrate another first down—a moving pocket play to buy time in case of a blitz. All that changed, though, when Doucet, recognizing the Sun Devils' switch to a zone, broke his route toward the goal line, prompting Russell to follow him to the left side of the field.

Fisher's yells filled the air. "STICK IT IN THERE!"

Russell knew what he was doing. "I eyeballed [Doucet], and he was working free. I kind of felt we had a chance at something great."

Just not yet.

Then he flung the ball, which fell into the outstretched arms of the diving, double-covered Doucet in a corner of the end zone.

The play dumbfounded even Fisher, who said the pass to Russell's left, was "… one very few guys in college could make—and very few in pro ball—and he stuck it 50 yards in the air on a line and made an unbelievable play."

That play also represented the fifth lead change of a 42-point fourth quarter.

JaMarcus Russell surveys his options.

Still, the coach questioned the quarterback. When Russell came to the sideline, Fisher told him the time to hit Doucet was when he made his break. Russell said the backside safety was moving into position to make a play, "Which I actually didn't see until I saw the film," Fisher said. "He was right; I was wrong. He made a terrific play on ability. We took a gamble, and it paid off."

The game wasn't over, and Arizona State used the remaining seconds to threaten one last time, reaching the LSU 28 before the defense—finally—held on four straight downs.

During a game that the Tigers had to overcome far more than fumbles and penalties, they had found a way to prevail.

* * *

That game kicked off a season in which the Tigers constantly overcame obstructions.

All things considered, it was one of LSU's most successful.

Somehow the Tigers won 11 of their 13 games (and no LSU team won as many games without finishing No. 1), were 5-1 in games decided by four or fewer points, and 3-1 in games decided by three or fewer points. They played in three overtime games, more than any other team in the country, and won two. Although LSU did not win the SEC, the Tigers won the SEC West for the third time in five years. On the field, LSU defeated four teams that finished in the top 17—the best performance in the country by that measuring stick. Only two other teams, national champion Texas and runner-up Southern Cal, won as many games against teams in the final AP Top 25.

That no college football team had overcome more hardship en route to a memorable season could be argued reasonably. Russell, thinking back to Arizona State, where he completed 16 of 29 passes for 242 yards, reflected:

"When I thought about how much so many people lost, I really thought that [bringing back a victory] was one thing that could cheer them up. It did, and I really feel good about it."

CHAPTER 28

MARCUS SPEARS

LSU 21 - Oklahoma 14
January 4, 2004 • New Orleans, Louisiana

Oklahoma's Heisman Trophy-winning quarterback, Jason White, dazed and befuddled after a half of being battered by a blur of white jerseys that just kept coming, dropped back and quickly threw the ball—right to LSU lineman Marcus Spears.

"It was like a gift when I saw it coming," Spears, who had dropped off the line, said. "I thought to myself, 'Get those hands up. The end zone's just ahead.'"

Spears lumbered 20 yards and, as he crossed the goal line, threw up his arm while holding the ball. On the second play of the second half, LSU had a two-touchdown lead over the favored Sooners at 21-7. It was the biggest play—the signature play—of the biggest game LSU played in more than four decades.

Oklahoma and the Tigers were in the Sugar Bowl vying for the Sears Trophy, emblematic of the national championship—at least the semi-official version sanctioned by the Bowl Championship Series, which was a coupling of polls and computer rankings that took into account pertinent factors. Oklahoma was No. 1 in the BCS standings, LSU No. 2; but in a game where the score was much closer than the action indicated, the Tiger defense was overwhelming the Sooners.

"Tigers are No. 1," says Marcus Spears after his touchdown against OU.

When he wasn't being sacked, White was being pressured and harried. Rarely, it seemed, would he throw a pass without geting at least touched by a Tiger lineman.

On the play before, the first after intermission, White was sacked for a four-yard loss by Spears, a 6 foot, 4 inch, 297-pound defensive end. The interception was, in part, a result of White's anticipation of the relentless LSU rush and defensive scheming. The Sooners didn't seem to know what was coming.

"At some points, I was lined up as a linebacker," Spears said. "Usually it was third-and-long situations. We have been doing it all season, not a lot, but we did it a lot tonight because they played empty [backfield] on offense."

LSU had a zone pressure call on when Spears made the interception and touchdown. "I don't think he ever saw me," Spears said later.

In a football battle of strength versus strength, Oklahoma entered the Sugar Bowl as the nation's highest scoring offense, averaging 45.2 points a game, while LSU was the defensive best in points allowed with an average of 10.8. The Tiger defense was clearly the superior unit in this matchup. After one quarter, the Sooners had a total of 50 yards; through three quarters, Oklahoma had 18 yards rushing on 21 attempts and just 61 yards passing—along with four sacks. The problem was—and it was a big one—Oklahoma stayed within reach of snatching away that mounted glass trophy on the sidelines, courtesy of the Tiger offense and special teams.

* * *

Pitting Oklahoma against LSU for the BCS championship was controversial, but not because of the Tigers, who were No. 2 in every poll and computer ranking. The Sooners—hovering at No. 1 for a record-tying 15 consecutive weeks and being called one of the greatest teams of college football history just a few weeks before—were upset by Kansas State 35-7 in the Big 12 championship game. Despite that defeat, OU's strength of schedule and its quality wins during the regular season kept them ahead of Southern Cal, which was No. 1 in the Associated Press poll, and LSU—two other teams with a lone loss.

LSU squeezed into the championship game largely on its strength of schedule, which was surprising. At the start of the season, the Tiger schedule seemed less imposing than normal. Virginia Tech backed out of its game in Baton Rouge in order to get an extra home date in Blacksburg, sending LSU scrambling. The Tigers then lured Louisiana-Monroe to Tiger Stadium, which put four so-called non-conference "weaklings" (Louisiana-Monroe, Western Illinois, Louisiana Tech, and Arizona) on LSU's 12-game regular-season schedule. Southern Cal was squeezed out of the championship game by its non-conference schedule of Auburn, Notre Dame, Brigham Young, and Hawaii. Those programs are often among the nation's best, but in 2003 went a combined 24-25.

Over the course of the season, LSU's foes began quietly building a case for the Tigers' quality opposition. The difference-making games, traced by the *New Orleans Times-Picayune*, started early:

- Louisiana Tech's stunning 20-19 victory at Michigan State on September 13—the Bulldogs were impressive in a comeback performance at the home of the Big Ten Spartans.
- Arkansas' 38-28 upset at Texas, also on September 13—the Longhorns finished No. 6 in the BCS standings and actually finished ahead of Oklahoma in the *New York Times* computer poll. The Razorbacks also beat Kentucky in seven overtimes on November 1 to help LSU's schedule strength.
- Washington's 28-17 loss at home to Nevada on October 11, which damaged USC. The Huskies were ranked in the preseason but finished 6-6—one of many disappointments in the Pac-10, which had a down season. Later, Washington hurt USC again by beating a Top-10 team in Washington State, taking away the Trojans' opportunity at a quality-win bonus.
- Ole Miss' 24-20 victory at Auburn on November 8—every one of the Rebels' nine wins was a boost for LSU, but this one came against one of USC's opponents, a double blow to the Trojans.
- Louisiana-Monroe's 45-42 victory at Louisiana-Lafayette on October 11—the Indians came though for the Tigers with their only win of the season, huge for LSU's strength of schedule rankings.

- Two games on the final day of the 2003 season finally determined the No. 2 berth in the title game: Boise State defeated USC opponent Hawaii, and Syracuse beat USC opponent Notre Dame.

All that, along with the Tigers' strong SEC schedule, which included two victories over Top-10 Georgia, factored the edging of USC in the BCS standings by 0.19 points—which equated to five places in the strength-of-schedule standings. There was little contrast between the two squads. USC had the more eye-catching offense, LSU an eye-raising and dominant defense. But the Tigers were in, the Trojans were out—though they remained No. 1 in the AP poll. Who had the stronger case? Seniors on the Arizona team said LSU was not only the best team they had played in 2003, but also the best team they played in their four years. Of course, Arizona's conference is the Pac-10, same as USC. Auburn coach Tommy Tuberville, whose team lost to USC 23-0 and to LSU 35-7, was diplomatic, saying both were outstanding—noting that USC's offense was playing at a very high level, but that LSU's defense was playing at an equally stratospheric plateau.

* * *

Oklahoma, favored by 6½ points, would have no such doubts. The Sooners had White, the nation's most decorated football player, a consensus All-American who passed for 3,744 yards and 40 touchdowns while completing 64 percent of his passes during the season. OU was also first in total defense, allowing 255.6 yards per game. The Sooners, befitting a squad once considered among the best ever, also collected seven major postseason individual awards, the most ever by one team.

LSU had but one consensus All-American, defensive tackle Chad Lavalais. The Tigers, though flying under radar in the nation's press, were brimming with talent. One of Nick Saban's goals when he became coach at LSU four years earlier was to corral the best Louisiana talent. He did, and for the previous two years was assessed to have the No. 1 recruiting classes in the country, including standouts such as defensive end Marquise Hill, cornerback Corey Webster, and Christian Life High

School teammates Michael Clayton, a receiver, and Spears, a tight end— both of whom thought they'd be playing at Miami.

Spears said he and Clayton were sold on staying home and helping Saban resurrect the football fortunes of LSU, which had gone 7-15 over the previous two seasons. The final selling point, according to Spears, was that Saban didn't promise him anything, even a starting job.

"He said he was going to play the best person at every position," Spears said. "Not every coach was that honest. I went to LSU, and he moved me to another spot, but it all worked out."

By the end of the 2003 season the Tigers, with Spears making his presence felt, were developing a calling card, leading the country in scoring defense. The defensive starters yielded just one rushing touchdown all year, and they themselves scored six times.

The Tigers were also stunning offensively, winning their last seven games by an average of 24 points. Lost in the pregame hoopla was one other little item: LSU quarterback Matt Mauck had a school-record 28 touchdown passes and actually had a better record as a starter (17-2) than White (15-2).

* * *

Justin Vincent, a redshirt freshman, set the tempo on the game's first play by popping up the middle, juking a linebacker five yards past the line of scrimmage, then galloping 64 yards to the OU 16. OU cornerback Derrick Strait barely prevented the touchdown by running him down. The Tigers fumbled at the goal line, though, but intercepted the ball just two plays later, setting up Skyler Green's 24-yard dance down the sideline for the game's first points.

OU then blocked a punt, recovering at the LSU 2-yard line, then punching into the end zone four plays later. Matt Mauck, throwing strikes, then led the Bengals on an 80-yard drive, finding Vincent again for an 18-yard touchdown capper.

That's where matters stood at the half, setting up Spears' heroics.

LSU, though, kept Oklahoma in the game. With a chance to go up by 17 in the third quarter, the Tigers erased a 27-yard field goal with *two* penalties on one play—10 for holding, 15 more for a personal foul.

Defensive end Marcus Spears left his mark at LSU.

Later, Mauck threw an interception that was returned to the LSU 30, eventually giving the Sooners their second touchdown. But the tiring Tigers weren't out of the woods. In the fourth quarter, the Sooners made their way inside the LSU 10, where the defenders stopped White on four straight pass attempts. On fourth-and-goal with 2:52 left, White went to OU's Mark Clayton, in the end zone. LSU freshman Jessie Daniels knocked the ball away. The game ended with White fittingly being sacked 52 yards from the end zone by linebacker Lionel Turner—the play Spears claims was the night's most important. Spears only acquiesced when reminded that his late-game interception represented the winning margin.

There was more than enough praise to go around. White finished with 13 completions in 37 attempts for 102 yards. He was sacked five times for minus-46 yards. The LSU defense held a team that averaged 461 yards over the season to 154 yards—52 of it rushing. LSU limited a team that averaged 45 points to 14, achieved on the short field provided by the Tigers. OU coach Bob Stoops said LSU was the best defense he'd seen in his five years as head coach in Norman.

* * *

Of course, LSU received its share of the national championship from the BCS, but Southern Cal stayed atop the AP poll. No one will ever know what might have happened if these two outstanding teams met, but Florida sportswriter Mike Bianchi, who had no personal favorite, left the Superdome convinced LSU deserved the top spot.

"After LSU's simmering 21-14 victory Sunday in this steaming gumbo pot of a stadium," Bianchi wrote:

> *I vote the Tigers No. 1 in the BCS (Bianchi Common Sense) poll. LSU (13-1) won one more game than USC (12-1); it played a tougher schedule; and the Tigers beat a better team (than Michigan) in their bowl game.*
> *Sure the Trojans are a great team. But so is LSU.*

Spears, surprisingly opted to return to LSU for his senior season, after which he became a No. 1 draft choice of the Dallas Cowboys.

"The thing I have to prove—and one of the things that I came back here to do—is leave a trademark at this school," Spears said after deciding to return. "I want to leave a stamp, make people remember me around here and remember these great teams and these guys."

No one with purple-and-gold loyalties could ever forget.

CHAPTER 29

JERRY STOVALL

LSU 10 - Georgia Tech 7
October 6, 1962 • Atlanta, Georgia

Jerry Stovall was huffin' and puffin', streaming down the middle of Grant Field, wondering why the goal posts at the other end didn't seem to get any closer.

"I just kept going and going," Stovall said, "and the uprights seemed to stay the same distance away. I thought I'd never make it."

As usual, though, he did. Ninety-eight yards from where Stovall took the second-half kickoff from Georgia Tech, he staked LSU to a lead in one of the most important games in Charlie McClendon's coaching career, in his first season after taking over for Paul Dietzel. The previous week two-touchdown underdog Rice tied LSU 6-6, giving McClendon a disappointing 1-0-1 record. The Tigers, expected to be a serious national-championship contender after returning most of their 1961 SEC Champion squad—were dropped completely out of the Top 10, a situation that rankled a segment of the LSU fan base.

"We really hadn't played as well as we could in the opening game against Texas A&M," Stovall recalled. "We struggled [despite scoring two second-half touchdowns for a 21-0 win], and we stunk it up in our second game. Georgia Tech was a real measuring stick for us."

Anyway you looked at it, this game was big, on national television at a time when only one college football game was shown—and no *SportsCenter* to show highlights. There were only a handful of postseason bowls, so worthy teams had to make their case on the field. One bad showing on TV could really ruin a season.

LSU needed that good showing to recover some of its national luster, but Tech wasn't going to make that easy. The favored Yellow Jackets, ranked No. 5 after impressive victories against Clemson and Florida were playing at home—a notorious spot for bad breaks and bad calls on visiting teams. Their outstanding offense included quarterback Billy Lothridge, halfback Joe Auer, and receiver Billy Martin, and the Tech lines were bigger and heavier than the Tigers. Tech was a showstopper team in those early days of television football, winning 10 of its 12 nationally televised games. LSU, with some of sports' most superstitious fans, wore purple jerseys for the first time in five years, an omen—as were daytime games, anathema for the night-prowling Bayou Bengals.

LSU's only source of momentum was its latent talent and Stovall— a lean, 6-foot-2, 195-pound senior with deceptive speed and a knack for making big plays.

Two years earlier, in his college debut against Texas A&M, Stovall kicked off in the second half. An Aggie return man eluded the first wave of Tigers, picked up a wall of blockers, and headed for the LSU goal. By midfield, only Stovall, the kicker, remained between the Aggie and the end zone. Backpedaling 30 yards, and fending off an A&M blocker the whole time without letting the runner get past him, Stovall was finally able to pin both against the sideline and made the tackle at the 20. A&M never did score in what was an eventual 9-0 LSU victory. The play caused Coach Paul Dietzel to say later, "Stovall's debut was as impressive as any I've seen by a sophomore."

That same season against three-touchdown favorite Ole Miss, Stovall had runs of 42 and 32 yards and averaged 44 yards on 10 punts during a memorable 6-6 tie that knocked the Rebels out of the national championship hunt. His key 57-yard run a year later defeated the

Jerry Stovall had a knack for making big plays.

unbeaten Rebels again in a classic 10-7 LSU victory. Against Kentucky, tied at 14-14, Stovall made a spectacular leaping reception that led to a field goal just before the half in a game LSU ultimately won 24-14. The point is: Jerry Stovall was a difference-maker, and to some a pleasant surprise.

* * *

Wearing his customary spectacles with his quiet disposition during the week, Stovall looked more like Clark Kent on campus than the Man of Steel he became on Saturdays.

Even though he was an All-State back at West Monroe High—the first that school ever produced—Stovall was the last prospect, the 52nd of a class of 52 signed by Dietzel in 1959. A.L. "Red" Swanson, a former LSU player, assistant coach, and at this time, a member of the school's Board of Supervisors, was the person who first saw something special in Stovall, and pushed for him.

"I think he may have held a gun to Coach Dietzel's head," Stovall joked before adding he wasn't sure he was anything close to being a prize recruit. Sheepishly he remembered being contacted by just three schools—Louisiana Tech, Tulane, and LSU—and seriously considered enrolling at hometown Northeast Louisiana University, where he could find employment while in school.

In view of what happened later, Stovall was simply overshadowed in a state that was flush with quality prospects at the time.

"Everywhere you looked in a hundred-mile radius [of West Monroe] in those days, there were just outstanding prospects," he said. "I always said I was the runt of the litter. I was very fortunate in the fact that Mr. Swanson first saw me play baseball as a ninth-grader, then followed my high school football career, and always seemed to think I had something. I could never thank him enough."

Swanson traveled with the youngster in his old Roadmaster from northern Louisiana to Baton Rouge five times to watch LSU games in 1958, Stovall's high school senior season, and, it turned out, a No. 1 season for the Tigers.

"I thought he would have to be redshirted a year, but he had the size, speed, and a great desire to play," Swanson recalled years later. "He had everything you could want."

Dietzel wasn't overwhelmed at first. "Jerry was among some very good football players we brought in at that time," Dietzel said. "He didn't stick out like a beacon, as John David Crow and Billy Cannon had done in previous years. But after he got here, it wasn't long before he moved to the top of the class."

Even his high school coach, Dan McClure, who coached Stovall in both football and baseball at West Monroe, said: "No one in their right mind would've figured him to be an All-American—unless they knew his temperament. You had to know what he had on the inside. When you did, you knew a person with that attitude would excel somewhere."

Yet, the person who may have spurred Stovall to football heights may have been his father. "It didn't take long at LSU," Stovall said, "to find out there were lots of bigger, faster, stronger players than me. I was discouraged, and called my dad and I told him I wanted to come home. He told me to come on home, that he'd help get me a job."

The elder Stovall worked as a salesman and had to rise at five in the morning to get started on his rounds.

"There wasn't a lot of sympathy there," Stovall said of his father who was working from dawn to dusk to make ends meet and who must have been irked listening to his boy complain about how difficult it had become to play a game.

"I thought about what he said, and the sound of his voice, for a minute," Stovall said. "Then I told Dad that maybe I'd give football a chance for a just a little longer."

* * *

Tech coach Bobby Dodd was acutely aware of the threat Stovall posed—he watched film of the Bengals' first game, in which Stovall trickily returned the ball 58 yards, setting up a touchdown. Sufficiently concerned, Dodd had Tech work all week on containing kickoffs.

The LSU scheme had a player—usually a quarterback—standing midfield on the 20-yard line with his back to the on-rushing enemy. The man taking the kickoff would run straight for that man in the middle, and when the timing was perfect, the return man would reach the quarterback just seconds before the kicking team did. The runner would either slip the ball to the quarterback who, in turn, would pitch back to another halfback cutting across left to right, or fake a handoff and head straight up field.

"It makes the other team come down a little cautious," explained McClendon, "and it also makes them cover from sideline to sideline."

Tech was perhaps too outside-conscious because—after faking to the up-man, Jimmy Field—Stovall shot up the field, veered to his left, where center Dennis Gaubatz blocked Lothridge twice to spring the play. Stovall set sail for the end zone, breaking into the clear at the LSU 40. The Xs and Os on Charlie Mac's blackboard practically came to life on the perfectly executed return.

"Two weeks ago, I faked the handoff against Texas A&M and almost got loose up the middle," Stovall said. "I think they expected something different this time. ... They were spread thin. I know I got a bunch of good blocks. ... I don't believe I ever saw daylight so soon—but I didn't think I had it until I put my foot in the end zone." Partly because Stovall felt like he was running in slow motion, in his mind, covering the length of the field seemed to take hours instead of seconds.

After that run, Stovall said his wife, Judy, said it was true: he had deceptive speed. "You're even slower than you look," he said Judy assessed.

When he caught his breath, Stovall suddenly became concerned. His father-in-law, W.C. Ward, had a heart attack a month before the game and was told not to attend or even listen to LSU games on the radio to avoid excitement.

"I hope my father-in-law is all right," Stovall said on the sideline. He was fine, but the Tigers weren't out of danger yet.

In the fourth quarter, Tech tied the score. On the ensuing kickoff, Charlie Cranford almost duplicated Stovall's run but was brought down on the Tech 48. Cranford fumbled, but LSU recovered and began a slow, arduous drive toward the Yellow Jacket end zone. The key play came on second-and-8 from the Tech 32, when quarterback Lynn Amadee flipped a pass to Stovall, who deftly sidestepped a tackler and went down to the 14.

"I hit Jerry quicker than we ordinarily do so our end would be in position to block their cornerback," recalled Amadee. "[Tight end] Billy Truax made a great block, and Jerry made a great run."

Four plays later, Amadee kicked a field goal that represented LSU's final points—in all of which Stovall played a major hand. Tech had a chance at a last-gasp victory when Auer got behind the LSU secondary at game's end, but he dropped the pass.

Even if Tech had snatched the victory, though, it really shouldn't have taken anything away from Stovall's heroics.

"In the second quarter," said Dr. Marty Broussard, then the Tiger trainer, "Jerry was hit hard. He came to the sideline, and when we checked him, we could feel he had a cracked rib. We put a pad on it and kept him out just six or seven minutes."

Then Stovall went back in, playing the rest of the game without missing a play on offense or on defense—one of many performances that moved Broussard, who had been at LSU as a student and trainer since 1938, to describe Stovall as "... the most respected man we've had around here in a long time."

* * *

At the end of the 1962 season, Stovall finished second in the balloting for the Heisman Trophy in what was then the closest vote for college football's most prestigious individual award. Terry Baker of Oregon State got 172 first-place votes and a total of 707 points to Stovall's 112 first-place votes and 618 total points. Stovall left LSU as a two-time All-American, with a 4.8 yards-per-carry career average. He also led the Tigers in receiving twice. McClendon put Stovall in focus, calling him "the most complete football player I've ever seen."

The next season, and for the following decade, Stovall applied his trade in the NFL. A first-round draft choice of the St. Louis Cardinals, Stovall had an All-Pro career as a safety. Afterward, in 1972, he went to work as an assistant for his old coach, Paul Dietzel, at the University of South Carolina. Then he returned to LSU as a McClendon aide.

Clearly, he aspired to become head coach at his alma mater, but those hopes seemed blunted. Most of the powers around LSU wanted a new beginning—and new names—after almost two decades under Charlie Mac, and Dietzel was brought in as AD to oversee and facilitate that change. Stovall went to work in a fund-raising capacity at LSU, and Dietzel lured North Carolina State head coach Robert "Bo" Rein.

But in one of the most bizarre incidents in Tiger history, 42 days later Rein and his pilot were killed in a plane crash after a recruiting trip. With no time to waste, Dietzel had to find someone capable enough and familiar enough with the Tiger program to take over immediately.

That person, of course, was Stovall.

The Stovall years at LSU were up-and-down seasons. Stovall steered the Tigers to the Orange Bowl in 1982, a year in which he was not only the SEC Coach of the Year but the Walter Camp National Coach of the Year as well. In 1983, however, the Tigers finished last in the SEC for the first time in history. That was the opening Bob Brodhead, who succeeded Dietzel as AD, needed to relieve an LSU football hero he hadn't hired.

After that Stovall became a bank vice-president, then, in 1990, accepted the athletic directorship at Louisiana Tech. Three years later, Stovall was back in familiar environs as president and CEO of the Baton Rouge Sports Foundation, where he remains today.

Even today, decades after he last donned a Tiger uniform, Jerry Stovall is a lasting symbol of Tiger achievement and tenacity. Perhaps the most incisive description of Jerry Stovall came from ex-teammate Tommy Neck, who served on the LSU Board of Supervisors at the time of the Rein tragedy.

"I've seen Jerry Stovall—in the fourth quarter when you're so tired you can hardly move and your lungs are burning—suck it up more than anyone else I've ever seen."

CHAPTER 30

JIM
TAYLOR

LSU 25 - Tulane 6
November 30, 1957 • Tiger Stadium

"With the ball under his arm," Paul Dietzel always maintains, "Jim Taylor was the best runner I've ever been associated with."

Taylor's cleat marks could be found on the backs of opposing jerseys throughout the South. In his two seasons as an LSU Tiger, he had many memorable performances:

- Four games into the '57 season, in 20-13 defeat of Georgia Tech, Taylor scored every Tiger point.
- Against Arkansas in 1956, Taylor rushed for 170 yards, spurring a 21-7 upset.
- In the same season, he scored LSU's lone touchdown, kicked the PAT, made a touchdown-saving tackle and had a late interception on the Tiger 8 as LSU beat Tulane 7-6.

In Dietzel's heart, nothing, though, could eclipse Taylor's heroics in his 1957 effort against the Green Wave, a contest played by two surprisingly mediocre teams. That watershed moment, though, has grown in importance over the years. Even Taylor said there was no inkling that this might be something special. "We were just preparing for a football game," he said. "Nothing more than that."

* * *

Taylor set the tone early, breaking loose for 48 yards and a touchdown on LSU's first possession.

"He didn't have much blocking," an account of the game read, "and he didn't need it. He just bounced off the few Tulanians who got a chance to stop him and carried on like a water buffalo."

Taylor bounced off tacklers all game on offense, scoring two touchdowns while gaining 171 yards—at the time, the second-best rushing total in Tiger annals. Then he turned around, when the Greenies had the ball, and bounced Tulane ball-carriers from his defensive spot at middle linebacker, which Taylor suspected was his best position. Tulane had just 10 first downs and 97 yards rushing.

It was a noteworthy performance. At the time, it didn't seem all that big, other than it was between these hated old antagonists. Tulane, after all, entered the fray with just a 2-7 record. The Tigers hadn't lost to the Wave in eight seasons, but in the last three games against Tulane, LSU sandwiched two one-point victories around a tie.

And an LSU victory would mean a 5-5 record, an improvement from the 3-5-2 and 3-7 slates in the first two years of the regime of Paul Dietzel, a young coach beginning to feel the heat from disgruntled fans. The Tigers started the season 4-1, then lost four in a row after an Asian Flu epidemic decimated the ranks of the thin Bengal roster.

"I probably wasn't smart enough to feel any pressure," Dietzel said. "But alumni are alike everywhere—they're not happy unless you're winning."

They were especially unhappy with a team that had a dream backfield. Taylor was on his way to an All-America season, and he was teamed with budding superstar halfback Billy Cannon and Johnny Robinson. The widespread virus, though, sidelined many of their blockers, a small fact LSU fans didn't seem to take into account.

Dietzel did have a pair of powerful allies, athletic director Jim Corbett, and university president General Troy Middleton, who hired Dietzel in 1955.

Jim Taylor—Once he got rolling, so did LSU.

In fact, Middleton wrote to Dietzel during the season, stating: "I heard there is some rumbling downtown, [that] there is unrest among the alumni; but I just wanted you to know that I am presently satisfied with the way you are running the football program, and I am [still] running this university."

"That," Dietzel said, "was something that really put iron in the back of a young coach."

* * *

The irony is that Dietzel had Taylor at all. He could have chosen many paths other than the LSU backfield. It took some time and the right set of circumstances.

The image of Jimmy Taylor playing football is one of a small bull churning his way up field with would-be tacklers bouncing off his sturdy legs of steel—the result of a hard childhood and an unwavering work ethic. His tremendous leg muscles were developed with two paper routes—one in the morning, the other in the afternoon—bicycling what he estimated to be "a million miles" for three dollars a week to help his widowed mother. Those legs, and his awesome athletic ability, could have taken him to the top of many sports.

"Jim could have played anything and been good at it," Bat Gourrier, once track and field coach at Baton Rouge High School, assessed. "If you stick a tennis racket in his hand, he would have been great. If someone had bought him a set of [golf] clubs, he could outdo you in that, too. He was just a natural athlete."

Between school and his paper routes, Taylor found time to develop into a hellacious *backcourt* player. "The first time I remember noticing Jimmy Taylor was when he played basketball," said Ted Castillo, the former prep editor of the *Baton Rouge Morning Advocate*. "He was an outstanding player and had a certain touch in his shooting."

In fact, Taylor didn't go out for the Baton Rouge High football team until he was a junior, when he stood 5 feet 9 inches and weighed 155 pounds. "I didn't like the game," Taylor candidly admitted. "I don't like anything unless I can do it real well."

He could play football really well, he eventually found.

At 5 feet 11 inches, 212 pounds, Taylor made state history when he became the first athlete to play in both the Louisiana All-Star football and basketball games.

He had a raft of scholarship offers in both sports, but opted for LSU and football—a sport to which he was acclimating. Clarence "Pop" Strange, who spent almost a half-century on the Tiger campus as a football assistant coach, said Taylor was "… probably the finest freshman athlete I've ever seen."

Jimmy had problems, and they weren't on the field. They were in the classroom. After a sterling freshman season, Taylor was routed to Hinds Junior College (Mississippi) to improve his grades. He did, and when he was eligible for major college competition again, he almost took a U-turn back to basketball. Taylor was seriously tempted to accept a round- ball offer from Miami, Colorado, or Furman. In the end, though, he decided his future was in football and at LSU—a program now under Dietzel.

Without benefit of spring practice, it took nearly a half season for Taylor to become acclimated to Dietzel's offense. Backfield coach Carl Maddox said LSU was simplifying its offense until Taylor became used to the new system. He played very well defensively, but Taylor—the heart of the Tiger attack—scored just eight points in LSU's first five games of 1956, all losses.

In the remaining five games of the season, Taylor broke loose, scoring 51 points to lead the SEC with 59, and LSU won three. If they hadn't, Dietzel might become nothing more than another footnote in LSU history books.

The next year, as LSU battled the Asian flu as well as 10 football opponents, Taylor led the SEC with 762 yards rushing and 86 points.

And he, as much as anyone, gave Dietzel—the man Taylor called "The Great White Father"—breathing room for his program. The Tigers had been 10-17-2 under Dietzel before that Tulane game. Afterwards they were 36-7-1, including the national championship of 1958, and the Tigers didn't experience a losing season for another 17 years.

"I can't say there was any idea by anyone that this game was more important than any other," Taylor, now largely retired from his Baton

Rouge real estate business and working to recover from a stroke, said, "It looks bigger now than it seemed at the time."

* * *

Taylor, of course, went on to an illustrious career with the Green Bay Packers. Even there, though, things turned out different than he expected. "Coming out of college, I thought I was a better linebacker than a fullback," Taylor reflected, "and I was told that's where I might play."

It took his pro experience for Taylor to even think of himself as a complete football player.

"Until Coach [Vince] Lombardi came to Green Bay, I had only been a running back for about 17 games," he said. "In high school, I played mainly defense until I was a senior. In junior college, I ran with the ball, but as a junior at LSU, it took me half a season to become effective. At LSU I didn't develop the skills necessary to become a pro running back. In college, I was running from tackle to tackle, did very little pass receiving and, really, very little blocking. I wasn't utilized that much."

He was utilized to the max, of course, under Lombardi, becoming *the* fullback prototype as Green Bay won four NFL championships and the first Super Bowl with Taylor in the lineup. He retired as the NFL's No. 2 career rusher with 8,597 yards, and is still ranked among the 25 best nearly 40 years later.

Taylor, who meant so much to Dietzel, meant a lot to Green Bay's legendary coach, too. He was the first of the Lombardi Packers to be enshrined in the Pro Football Hall of Fame.

CHAPTER 31

Y.A.
TITTLE

LSU 27 - Alabama 27
September 30, 1944 • Tiger Stadium

The passer dropped back, scanned the field, then let fly to a receiver who momentarily broke free.

According to one account, "Y.A. Tittle, freshman passer extraordinaire, whipped the ball 30 yards to wingback Dan Sandifer, who took it on the 4 and staggered over [the goal line]."

A star was born.

It was the first game of what would become an illustrious collegiate and professional career, and the 17-year-old Tittle proved something— to himself. He played well enough—in the season opener against an Alabama team that would finish the year in the Sugar Bowl—to show his name belonged among the star-spangled rosters of the combined squads.

"I wasn't sure I should be out there," Tittle said. "Some of those guys like [fellow LSU freshmen] Sandifer, Ray Coates, Jim Cason, [sophomores Gene] 'Red' Knight, and Elwyn Rowan were really great backs, and we were playing against outstanding Alabama people like Harry Gilmer. I had a lot of doubt about my abilities compared to theirs."

He belonged. It's an intriguing note in Tiger annals to realize that future Pro Football Hall of Fame running back Steve Van Buren left LSU in 1943 and future Pro Football Hall of Fame quarterback Tittle entered LSU in 1944.

The game itself wasn't a barometer of what was to come. Tittle played second string, though he threw LSU's only touchdown pass—a second-quarter pass that gave the Tigers a 14-7 lead—in the thrilling 27-27 tie. Individual passing statistics weren't carried in newspapers then and aren't available today, but team stats were and show that the Tigers completed 8-of-13 passes for 103 yards and one touchdown. It is recorded that Tittle did throw an interception.

It is fair, though, judging from the observer's comments, to believe Tittle must have been responsible for some of LSU's passing acumen.

He also ran eight times for a net of 16 yards, returned three punts for 46 yards, had eight punts for a 32-yard average—three of which expertly went out inside the Bama 10—and on defense temporarily saved a touchdown by tackling Gilmer at the goal line.

It sounds like a routine outing for a young single-wing tailback on a rebuilding LSU team that would win just two games in 1944.

"Not really," said Tittle, the CEO of Y.A. Tittle and Associates, a San Francisco-area insurance concern. "That game gave me confidence, eased the doubts I had about playing with the great athletes that were on that field that night."

"Y.A. was always a hard worker," said Ray Coates, who was moved to halfback the next season when LSU installed the T-formation to take advantage of Tittle's passing skills. "He was good at the start of the [1944] season. But he was excellent at the end."

While the young Tigers were learning, they were taking some hard lessons losing four games by a total of 23 points and beating only Georgia before the finale against Tulane. Tittle, who was getting better and better, blossomed against the Green Wave, completing 13-of-17, including his first 12 in a row as LSU won 25-7. It would take nearly 50 years for a Tiger quarterback to exceed Tittle's school record for consecutive completions.

Said Coates simply, "Y.A. was almost perfect that day."

* * *

Tittle, of course, was one of the finest quarterbacks ever to play at LSU—ever to play anywhere for that matter.

Y.A. Tittle showed he belonged from the start.

Football fever struck Tittle in the same way, and at the same time, it struck hundreds of youngsters in the late 1930s, through a national rage named Sammy Baugh, who was changing the role of quarterbacks at Texas Christian University. Baugh made the forward pass an integral part of the sport, as important as running and blocking. As a school boy in Marshall, Texas, Y.A. became obsessed with Baugh and his style of play. "I did everything the way I thought Baugh would do it," Tittle said, "even to the point of throwing footballs through tire loops. I had seen Sammy do that in newsreels. I don't think running ever crossed my mind."

Interestingly, the Tigers landed this passing protégé in large part because of his older brother, who was an All-SEC player at Tulane.

"Every year," Y.A. recalled, "we'd go see Jack play against LSU, and I was impressed even as a young kid with the enthusiasm, the tiger in the cage, the campus, just the whole LSU atmosphere. I was recruited by a number of schools, but I wanted LSU; and I committed to LSU right after my senior season. But I got so much pressure from the people in Marshall about going to a Texas school that I finally agreed to visit the University of Texas. I went down there and after a week of, shall we say, 'good recruiting,' I agreed to attend Texas."

Given a summer job in Austin, Tittle quickly became a bit disenchanted with the lifestyles of some of the big-city Texas kids on campus, including his roommate, Bobby Layne. "He was so far ahead of me [socially], him being from Dallas," Tittle said with a cringe. "It wasn't even funny. At that point of my life, I had never even had a taste of beer, and he was already playing no-limit poker and running around with all the gals in Austin, boozing it up and having just a helluva good time. I guess I felt a bit inadequate. And every morning I had to listen to ol' Bobby's stories of conquest."

Three weeks after Tittle went to Austin, LSU assistant Red Swanson had breakfast with the youngster, who had not yet actually enrolled at Texas. Swanson asked Y.A. if he'd like to change his mind.

"I said I would, but I felt embarrassed about it," Tittle said. "But Swanson said it was okay as long as I called Coach [Dana] Bible and told him."

Swanson said he'd have no hand in taking the boy off campus without Bible's knowledge; and it was, after all, his own decision. The unhappy youngster went to a phone booth, faked a call, pretended to be talking, then walked out and told Swanson, "Everything seems to be okay."

Swanson and Tittle made one stop in Houston to pick up another prospect, and the three sped straight to Baton Rouge. Four years later, Y.A. left behind a fistful of records (including 2,525 yards passing and 23 touchdown passes, pretty gaudy stats for the era), most of his hair, and a lingering legend.

Known as the Bald Eagle throughout his notable professional career, Tittle began losing his hair at a young age. Trainer Herman Lang explained years later that, in college, Tittle felt his helmet had something to do with his receding hairline.

"Y.A. always wanted to put something in his helmet. He was sure that was the reason he was losing his hair."

Tittle later thought an LSU tradition of shaving freshmen heads may have had an influence. "I had the ugliest-looking scalp. I'm not sure it didn't just stunt my hair growth because it sure never came back the right way."

His name was another sore spot aggravated by LSU. Publicist Jim Corbett recognized a story angle. "Coach Bernie Moore," Corbett once explained, "allowed me each day at the beginning of September practices to meet with a dozen of his football players for the purposes of processing personnel data, and I vividly remember first meeting Y.A. I asked him to fill out his full name—initials were not enough.

"He responded with 'That's my name, my full name.' Curious, I checked with the registrar's records and found that, indeed, his application carried the initials and not a first name. I was satisfied for the moment. For the next few days, I saw him work at quarterback under the newly installed T-formation. It was evident that here was a tremendous passer, if not a great quarterback, and the wheels of curiosity began to roll.

"I left the field and returned to my office and called the courthouse at his home in Marshall, Texas, and requested information on one Y.A. Tittle. There was no one by that name in the record book, the voice answered, but 'We do have a Yelberton Abraham Tittle.' The next day I called Y.A. in and asked him if he had ever seen this name before. He said, 'I'd appreciate it if you lay off using my name.'

"Instead I laid it on as football's most exciting name—and as it turned out at LSU, its greatest T-formation passer and quarterback."

* * *

The T-formation was overtaking football at the time, but Tittle probably forced Coach Bernie Moore to go to it earlier than he would have preferred. Moore liked his single-wing, but the tailback in that offense had to be able to run and throw. Tittle could only do one.

"I was so slow that, when I ran," Tittle said, "opponents thought it was a fake—a slow developing fake."

Moore moved Tittle to quarterback in the new offense and moved Coates to halfback to take continued advantage of his running ability, and, in an odd bit of strategy, to have him call the plays. In an era when 10 passes a game would have been considered an aerial circus, Moore was circumventing a potential problem.

"If Y.A. called the plays," Cason said with a chuckle, "every play would have been a pass."

With Tittle under center, LSU put together a couple of sterling seasons (7-2-0 in 1945 and 9-1-1 in 1946) and recorded some memorable victories.

In '45, the underdog Tigers ventured to Athens and beat Georgia and Charlie Trippi 32-0.

Tittle engineered a late drive in Atlanta as LSU beat Georgia Tech for the first time, 9-7. In '46, in perhaps the game of that year in the South, Tittle outdueled Gilmer as the Tigers beat 'Bama, 31-21.

Following the season, in the original Ice Bowl—in below-freezing temperatures in the Cotton Bowl—Tittle guided the Bayou Bengals to 15 first downs (Arkansas had just one), and 271 total yards (Arkansas had just 54). The shivering Tigers, however, were unable to score in a 0-0 deadlock, although they penetrated the Arkansas 10-yard line five times.

"Probably the most complete game I had at LSU was that Tulane game of 1944," Tittle said. "Everything went right in that game. I honestly don't think, though, that I could have performed that well in November had I not done a good enough job to build my confidence against Alabama in September. That game meant everything to me."

* * *

However, the single play for which Tittle will be remembered forever at LSU came on defense, and has become part of the lore of Southeastern Conference football. Charlie Conerly and Tittle were locked in a '40s version of an aerial circus in the 1947 Ole Miss-Tiger encounter.

In the fourth quarter, Conerly hit a receiver in the flat. It bounced off the receiver's chest. Tittle cut in front and intercepted at the LSU 15. "He was sort of holding me from my rear, around my belt," Tittle said, "and when he pulled, it snapped my belt buckle loose."

Tittle was in the clear, 70 yards from the goal, holding the ball in his right arm, his pants with his left arm.

The legend is that Tittle's pants slipped to his knees, but apparently that is not what really happened. A newspaper account said Tittle "... almost lost his pants on the run as his belt broke."

Barney Poole, one of the Rebels who stopped Tittle on the 38-yard line, preserving Ole Miss' 20-18 victory, said there was one thing about the incident that has never been cleared up.

"Coach [Johnny] Vaught taught us a lot of football," Poole said years later. "But he never did teach us where to throw the head when tackling a man losing his pants."

CHAPTER 32

HERB TYLER

LSU 28 - Florida 21
October 11, 1997 • Tiger Stadium

It was something like the Rapture. With the exuberant crowd, many poised on the chain-link fence surrounding the field at Tiger Stadium ready to storm the goal posts as they counted down the final seconds, a feeling of pure and unadulterated joy swept through Herb Tyler.

"Just the greatest feeling God can fill a human with is what went through me," Tyler said in describing his emotions after quarterbacking LSU to a momentous victory. "It was a moment I'll never forget."

And a moment that will be remembered forever in Tiger Town. LSU had beaten two formidable opponents on that one memorable night: (1) annual SEC antagonist and defending national champion Florida; (2) history.

In more than a century of playing football before this evening, LSU had played eight opponents ranked No. 1 to no avail. The Tigers were 0-7-1 in such encounters. The ninth try was, finally, the charm.

A masterful game plan put in by Coach Gerry DiNardo, executed almost flawlessly by Tyler on offense and by a pack of Tigers defensively, erased that ignoble record.

"We won that game during the week," Tyler said, referring to the Xs and Os drawn up in the Tigers' meeting rooms in the days leading up to the Gators. "We were prepared, and we were ready."

Far easier said than done against any quality opponent, but the idea on offense was to smack Florida in the mouth, to attack the Gators in the middle of the line, to involve the fullback as much as possible. In that regard, LSU put in two simple power plays: a new trap and a new belly play.

Guard Alan Faneca explained later: "The coaches told us before the game that we were more physical than they were. We were the more physical team. If we pushed them off the ball, we could create holes. That would enable us to pass the ball. We executed everywhere we needed to."

LSU rushed 38 times for 158 yards with workhorse Kevin Faulk gaining 78, and fullback Tommy Banks carrying five times for 34 yards and one touchdown. Almost all the plays were drawn up with jabs at the center of the line. Tyler, a mobile quarterback, was a bonus, gaining 50 yards with two touchdown runs in addition to 10 completions in 17 passing attempts for another 172 yards.

On defense, the Tigers reached back into their own history, back to the famed backup defensive unit, the Chinese Bandits. The LSU staff knew it had to do something radical in order to slow the Fun 'n' Gun Gator offense, which was flattening opposing defenses to the frightening tune of 476.2 yards a game and 49.4 points. That would be a major concern.

To keep their defensive starters fresh and still keep pressure on Gator quarterback Doug Johnson, DiNardo and his staff revived the concept of the Bandits and identified a core of six line and linebacker reserves good enough to weave among the regulars without seriously hurting the effort.

Defensive coordinator Carl Reese came up with the idea while watching the tapes of Florida's 56-7 victory over Arkansas the previous week. The Razorbacks hit Johnson 16 times, got two sacks, and forced four scrambles. "They had the right idea," said Reese. "The problem was their good players wore down. We wanted to get enough bodies in to chase the quarterback. Fresh legs and fresh minds can make it happen for you."

They certainly did on this night.

The Bandit package sacked Johnson five times, intercepted him four times, and limited Florida to 49 rushing yards. Johnson threw for 346 yards, but for the first time in 62 regular-season games, the Gators were not able to hit a touchdown pass.

Everything, as it turned out, worked well, a major surprise not only to the sporting public but also to LSU fans. The Tigers in general and Tyler in particular were in disfavor after LSU struggled to a 7-6 win over Vanderbilt the week before—a game that would have been an embarrassing defeat if not for a blocked field goal in the fading seconds.

Still, LSU was 4-1 entering the game against the Gators, 5-0 and winners of their last 26 SEC games.

"Listen, we were capable," Tyler said, "and we had a reason to play hard and stay focused."

Very good reason.

* * *

Any team ranked No. 1, of course, at least at the time of the polls, has serious credentials, and there's no disgrace in falling short against such an opponent. Several times LSU came frustratingly close to knocking off a team perched atop the polls, but never were the Tigers able to light the cigar.

Against Nebraska, in the season-opener of 1976, a last-play 44-yard LSU field goal missed by inches, leaving the Tigers with a 6-6 deadlock.

Two teams ranked No. 1 showed up in Tiger Stadium in 1979, with powerful Southern Cal played off its cleats in a 17-12 victory decided in the last minute. Alabama squeaked by in a 3-0 Crimson Tide victory played in rain and mud.

Florida State got a major scare in 1991 when the Tigers, in the middle of a 5-6 season and a three-touchdown underdog, took a 16-7 halftime lead only to lose 27-16. It's written in the book *Saint Bobby and the Barbarians* that Seminoles coach Bobby Bowden was beside himself afterward, saying, "That was one of the greatest wins Florida State ever had."

Herb Tyler spurred the Tigers to a long-awaited win over No. 1 Florida.

These are the results of LSU vs. No. 1-ranked opponents:

November 4, 1939	Tennessee	0-20
November 5, 1955	Maryland	0-13
September 11, 1976	Nebraska	6-6
September 29, 1979	Southern Cal	12-17
November 10, 1979	Alabama	0-3
October 26, 1991	Florida State	16-27
October 8, 1994	Florida	18-42
October 12, 1996	Florida	13-56
October 11, 1997	Florida	28-21

In its last two games against Florida, LSU could have played the Gators from then to now and never taken a lead. Florida was that superior. But the Tigers also felt that, under point-happy coach Steve Spurrier, the Gators enjoyed rubbing LSU's collective nose in the dirt, particularly in the 1996 game in which the Gators bagged the Tigers 56-13.

"Long after things were settled, they still wanted more [points]," Tyler said. "It was an embarrassing game, and we remembered that."

* * *

The first jersey issued to Herb Tyler at LSU was No. 41.

"That's not a quarterback number," Tyler, now a project manager and estimator for a home construction company in New Orleans, said. "I was a quarterback all my career, and that's where I wanted to play in college. I think they saw me as a defensive back."

What the Tiger coaching staff really saw in DiNardo's first recruiting excursion was a spirited athlete with skills that could help anywhere on the squad. The coaches saw a kid who guided his O.P. Walker High in New Orleans to the first round of the 1994 state playoffs and played the grueling game with such intensity and energy that he missed the game's conclusion, aided to the sidelines because of exhaustion.

LSU knew what kind of kid and athlete he was. Where he would play was the question. At 5 feet, 10 inches, 183 pounds, Tyler would be at a disadvantage in seeing over the line at quarterback.

"Coach DiNardo called me in and told me the decision would be mine, but that he thought it would be in my best interest to consider moving to the secondary. I said I'd rather kneel, watch, learn, and be ready at quarterback when he needed me."

Now wearing No. 14, Tyler started the season fourth on the depth chart, but moved up by the eighth game against North Texas. He greatly impressed DiNardo when he ran the scout squad the week of the Rice game, four weeks into the season, giving the defense a good look at the Owls' triple option. When Jamie Howard went down with an injury, Tyler further impressed the coaches with sterling performances in wins against Ole Miss (38-9) and Arkansas (28-0), then Michigan State (45-26) in the Independence Bowl.

Tyler gave LSU a different look. Howard was more a traditional drop-back passer, Tyler was a mobile runner whose constant movement created passing lanes—but he could throw from the pocket as well.

"I love the way the kid sets up to throw the slant," said one observer with the qualifications to judge. "You say he's how old? Eighteen? All I know is, it took me a long time to throw that kind of pass," said Y.A. Tittle. "It takes talent. That kid is a real find."

After Tyler's freshman year, DiNardo assessed, "Sometimes he tries to do too much." But he added, "I like his competitiveness, and I like his composure."

By the time Tyler took the field against Florida in 1997, he had accumulated an 18-3 record as a starter.

* * *

From the start, it was an LSU night. On the Tigers' first possession, they coasted to the Gator 16, where a fumble blunted the drive. They came right back after Florida punted to Kevin Faulk, who returned it to the Gator 40. On the first play, Tyler, running the option, faked a pitch to Faulk then cut inside and shot down the field through an empty secondary to the end zone.

Herb Tyler, a nimble runner, gave LSU a different look.

"The defensive end didn't seem to know what to do; and in that instant of hesitation, I took off," Tyler recalled.

Three plays later, Cedrick Donaldson got the first of LSU's interceptions and returned it 68 yards to the Florida 7, leading to the Tigers' second touchdown and a startling 14-0 lead, which is how the quarter ended. There was significance in that. Florida had outscored its previous five opponents 91-3 in the opening period.

Of course, Florida came back, tying the score at 14. This, however, was one of those magical Tiger nights. In a span of 93 fourth-quarter seconds, LSU put up 14 more points—ignited by the same players responsible for the first-period pyrotechnics.

Donaldson again picked off Johnson and brought it back 31 yards for a touchdown with 11:40 to play. Florida fumbled the ensuing kickoff, and LSU recovered at the Gator 30.

Four plays later, Tyler ran another option, again keeping and this time going 12 yards for the touchdown.

"The defender stayed between me and Kevin," Tyler said. "I just took off, right behind Alan Faneca. I knew no one was going to get through him to me."

Trying to run out the clock, LSU had a third-and-6 with 1:50 remaining. On a comeback route, Tyler speared receiver Abram Booby, who bobbled the ball, 15 yards down field. "'Don't drop that thing!' I was yelling," Tyler said. "But he had great hands, an exceptional pass catcher, and he made the play, maybe the biggest play of the game."

Banks, like his teammates, said the game plan powered the Tigers to their first victory over a No. 1-ranked opponent.

"We'd hit in there in a hole over the guard, then use the same play in another hole over tackle. When they started bringing their defensive backs up—and the safeties close to the line with eight or nine in box—our play-actions just opened up.

"You know, that game was played almost exactly the way the coaches drew it up."

CHAPTER 33

JACOB HESTER

LSU 28 - Alabama 24
October 6, 2007 • Tiger Stadium

Like the human pile-driver he'd been all night, Jacob Hester, groaning and grunting, body inches from the ground, shot into the middle of the line, through a wall of defenders and into the end zone.

That two-yard run with 1:09 remaining, was the defining play in what every one of the 92,910 spectators on hand knew at the time was an instant classic. No. 1-ranked LSU and defending national champion Florida went toe-to-toe for 60 minutes and the Tigers emerged with a scintillating victory.

That night Hester took his place in the pantheon of Tiger heroes.

The statistics weren't stupendous, 106 yards on 23 carries and a touchdown, but Tiger coach Les Miles marveled that Hester, who also played on special teams, turned in one of the best all-around performances he'd seen in 30 years of coaching. Others were similarly impressed. Hester was named National Back of the Week in what was obviously college football's game of the week.

Who would've thought it? A fullback/tailback said to be too small (5-foot-11) and too slow (4.540) to excel at this level, Hester said wryly, "I've always heard I'm not the biggest or the fastest." There were those, many, who echoed those thoughts, quick to criticize Miles for starting Hester over some of the backups in his stable.

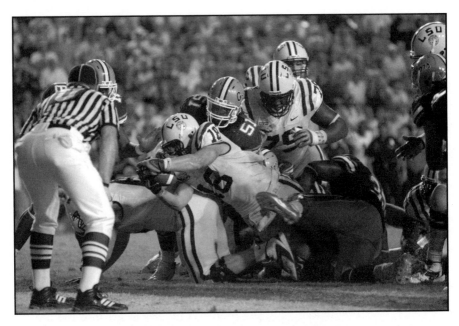

Jacob Hester scores with 1:09 remaining to complete LSU's comeback victory over Florida on October 6, 2007.

But Miles knew the heart of his 2007 backfield, his blue-collar thoroughbred, was the complete package, what is admiringly called in coaching circles as strictly "a football player." As a senior, Hester spent time on the Tigers kickoff coverage, punt coverage, punt returns, extra point and field goal teams, as well as his backfield duties. As the top back in LSU's five-man rotation, he led the team in rushing attempts (225), yards (1,103), average (4.9) and touchdowns (12) to go with 14 receptions for 106 yards and another touchdown.

* * *

Miles knew he'd need Hester at his best and a few more Tigers to play above their capabilities—plus install some unconventional strategy in the LSU playbook—to catch Florida off-stride and have a chance against the physical No. 9-ranked Gators.

"We knew this was going to be rough," Hester recalled. "Plenty tough."

The week before the Gators lost 20-17 to Auburn on the last play of the game. No Urban Meyer-coached team had lost two straight games for five years.

Emerging superstar quarterback Tim Tebow was beginning to make his legitimate, and ultimately successful, case as the first sophomore worthy of the Heisman Trophy. Although LSU statistically had the nation's best defense, Hester said no one was fooled. "We knew we had our hands full."

Maybe this would be important, maybe not, but LSU would be playing before a national prime-time television audience with the additional burden of playing at the pinnacle of the polls for the first time since 1959. The Tigers had won the 2003 BCS national title, but were never ranked No. 1 until after the title game.

Miles felt he would need all hands on deck, ready to give their all.

Hester was ready, putting on his earphones to get into the proper frame of mind. *"Deep in my heart there's a trembling question. Still I am sure the answer's gonna come somehow."*

Hours before kickoff the message was coming through loud and clear. The smoky, intense voice reassured him, transmitted to Hester in equal shots of adrenalin and inspiration. The King always had that effect on him

Elvis Presley has been described as *the* singer of the 20th Century. This, however, was the 21st Century. Hester was a throwback, as comfortable in the pop-culture of America of 50 years ago as some of his LSU teammates were in the hip-hop rage of the day with, say, Snoop Dog.

In any case, properly motivated by Presley's gospel-tinged rendition of *If I Can Dream*, Hester had one thought for the pivotal moment of LSU's season: Game on.

* * *

Oh, oh. This was going to be even worse than anyone thought. Tebow was near-unstoppable, LSU's vaunted defense, giving up just

174.6 yards a game going in, was on its heels almost all night as the Gators three times built 10-point leads (10-0, 17-7, 24-14).

Early on, the Tigers couldn't get the ball away from Florida, which ran 21 plays to LSU's 10 in the first quarter, and out-gained their hosts 87-45. That trend began changing in the second as LSU began finding creases in the Gators line, and began playing with more assurance— which would only increase as the game went on.

No one knew it at the time, but backup quarterback Ryan Perrilloux's 1-yard touchdown run in the second period, cutting Florida's lead to 10-7, was a preview of Miles' strategy. Eschewing a field goal, Miles gambled on fourth down that his team could make a yard—and place an element of doubt on Florida's sense of invincibility.

* * *

Jacob Hester was a walking stereotype, born and raised with old school values and tastes. Growing up in Shreveport the son of Joey and Nancy, a pair of pretty fair athletes in their own rights, he was surrounded by their influences: Presley, Dean Martin, and the Duke, John Wayne. All three of the Hester boys were named for characters from Wayne movies. Jacob was named for Wayne's 1971 film *Big Jake*.

"I guess I was born a little too late," he said. "You just don't see a lot of guys with the same kind of interests that I have. I guess I am a little bit of an oddball in that sense. But it's been working in the way I play football. It's an honor being called an old-school football player."

Originally a nose guard for Evangel Christian, when the team's starting tailback was sidelined, assistant coach Chris Tilley lobbied for Jacob to fill in. He responded with a game of more than 200 yards and finished with a season total of 1,593 for the state champions. "You should have seen him then, playing at 250 pounds because he'd been a nose tackle," Tilley recalled of the time when the beefy Hester earned the nickname 'Freight Train.' You talk about seeing someone run over people. It was really something."

The coach profoundly altered the course of Hester's life, since he is also the father of Katie, to whom Jacob, after first getting approval from

Tilley, proposed after the 2006 regular-season-ending Arkansas game. The proposal was accepted.

Old school, to say the least.

Still, as an LSU player Hester often brought double-takes. It went against cultural biases to see a white guy being the dominant back on a national championship-contending college football team. In a 2006 game against Tennessee, during a first-quarter timeout when he took off his helmet, a shocked Vols linebacker Jerod Mayo said to Hester, "Shouldn't you be playing at Air Force?"

Even the denizens sitting in Tiger Stadium second-guessed Miles for not playing backups over Hester. There were pictures in the Hester household of his best friends at LSU, including backs Keiland Williams and Charles Scott, both African-Americans. But the veiled stereotypical remarks bothered his mom. Talking about it once, she said, "I hear and see it all the time that he's not fast enough. And sometimes it makes me want to yell, 'What you really want to say is that he's white.'"

Keiland and Charles burst out laughing about their friend's circumstance.

Hester claimed with his customary aplomb, the perception was no big deal, "That never bothers me. As far as I'm concerned, that's an advantage for me. Let 'em think that.'"

* * *

The Tigers unlocked the secret to beating Florida—keep the ball away from Tebow. Easier said than done, but it brought on the strategy that would brand Miles as "The Mad Hatter."

In the third quarter, with the score 17-7, the Tigers were lined up for a field goal attempt on fourth-and-five. The holder, quarterback Matt Flynn, took the snap, jumped up and ran for an eight-yard gain. The first down eventually led to LSU's second touchdown.

Tebow came right back with a 75-yard scoring drive in five plays to put LSU behind by two scores again as the fourth quarter began, buttressing Miles' plan of doing all he could to keeping the ball out of Tebow's hands.

In the final 15 minutes, the Gators would gain just 37 yards, turn over the ball twice—and give three more, crucial, fourth down plays to the Tigers.

A Tebow pass was tipped and defensive end Kirsten Pittman, saying he saw a "pot of gold" hovering against the lights of Tiger Stadium, intercepted at the Florida 27. Florida slowed the LSU advance near the goal, but, going for it again on fourth and three at the Gator four, Flynn scrambled to his right and hit wideout Demetrius Byrd for the touchdown that cut the score to 24-21.

Already having an effective night, events would now turn the remaining 10 minutes into Hester Time.

After stopping the Gators cold—finally—on a three-and-out, LSU went on a memorable 60-yard, eight-minute drive.

A penalty put LSU in a deep hole, and Flynn scrambled for 15 yards on third down, making it fourth-and-one. Going for it, of course, Hester plowed into the stacked Florida line for a two-yard gain and the first down. Moments later on a second-and-long, he broke away and reaching the secondary, lowered his head and took Gator safety Major Wright for a ride on his 19-yard run, electrifying his teammates.

But it embarrassed Wright, who gave Hester a parting verbal shot. "As we were getting up," Hester recalled, "Wright's like, 'That's all right. You still look like Vanilla Ice.' I was like, 'Aw, Vanilla Ice? That's the lowest blow.'"

Several plays later, LSU once again stared at fourth down, this time at the Gator 7 with almost two yards to go. Hester made it with inches to spare. That set up the two-yard bolt into the end zone that Hester will forever be remembered for in Tiger-town, absorbing another ferocious tackle but squeezing into the end zone. Then lying prone on the turf as his jubilant teammates went wild on the sideline.

What will also be remembered from that game is Miles' play-calling. LSU went for it five times on fourth down, and made it each time—a strategy without which the Tigers could not possibly have prevailed. Here was the breakdown:

4-1 at Florida 1, Perrilloux, 1 yard run, TD, (second quarter);

4-5 at Florida 25, Flynn, 8-yard run (led to TD), third quarter;

4-3 at Florida 4, Flynn 4-yard pass to Byrd, TD, fourth quarter;

4-1 at LSU 49, Hester 2-yard run (led to TD), fourth quarter;

4-1 at Florida 7, Hester 2-yard run (led to TD), fourth quarter.

What is not recalled is that they were not gambles as much as calculated risks. During the 2007 season LSU converted on 45 percent of its third-down plays (93-of-205), an NCAA best 12-of-15 (80 percent) on fourth down, and 73.1 percent (19-of-26) when Hester carried in either situation needing four or fewer yards.

"The point is we couldn't give them the ball," Miles said. "And we had the weapons to keep the ball."

* * *

The point was valid. Tebow had a hand in 220 yards of the 314 his team gained (67 rushing, 158 passing), and perhaps the game's most telling stat was time of possession. LSU had the ball for 35:52, Florida 24:08, more than 10 critical minutes difference when Tebow couldn't do his damage.

"Those two turnovers we had killed us," he said in the locker room, "but you have to give LSU credit. I like the way Coach Miles went for it on fourth down. He's a gambler, just like Coach Meyer. He's out there to win."

He was, and LSU went on from there to the national championship. But then, he had one of most resourceful teams LSU ever fielded.

After Hester's touchdown tumble set off a seismic celebration in LSU's concrete valley, he lay on his back clutching his right knee in apparent anguish. But he wasn't hurt. Something lodged in his chinstrap, preventing him from buckling his helmet. Fixing the problem in time for Hester to line-up for his blocking duties on the ensuing PAT would have almost certainly resulted in a penalty.

Rather than burn the Tigers' remaining timeout, Hester followed his first instinct and played possum. While he was being helped off the field during an injury stoppage, LSU sent in a sub, and the successful extra point attempt went off without a hitch.

A last, desperate Tebow pass was batted down harmlessly in the end zone, signaling the end to one of those magical games that will replayed mentally by Tiger fans for years to come . . . a Golden Oldie.

CHAPTER 34

JORDAN JEFFERSON

LSU 41 - Texas A&M 24
January 7, 2011 • Dallas, Texas

In a feast-or-famine season, Jordan Jefferson was figuratively gorging himself on the Texas Aggies.

Jefferson not only ignited LSU to a season-high 446 yards against one of the better defenses in college football, but he also threw three touchdown passes.

For a quarterback who threw just four touchdown passes in a 12-game regular season, that was a fairly satisfying outing.

"I was pretty happy with my game," the taciturn Jefferson admitted. "I believe I kind of showed something to the critics."

Indeed. In a short 60-playing minutes span in the AT&T Cotton Bowl against Texas A&M, Jefferson went from being perceived by some as a millstone holding the Tigers back to the firing pin of a potent offense.

"I thought he was a complete quarterback," said one of the game's most interested observers, A&M coach Mike Sherman. "I thought he was decisive, aggressive and accurate. He snuck a couple in there that I didn't think were going to get in."

High praise for a man at the helm of the nation's 107th passing offense, and who was college football's 92nd most efficient starting quarterback.

Jordan Jefferson jump-started LSU's dormant offense in the Cotton Bowl.

Those rankings would make anyone wonder how LSU could possibly finish with an 11-2 record and fall just 15 points short of an unbeaten season—and a possible berth in the BCS national championship game.

Would the real Jordan Jefferson please stand up?

He did in the season opener against North Carolina, a team depleted by accusations of academic fraud, throwing for two touchdowns in the first half of a 30-24 squeaker.

Then he didn't have another touchdown pass in LSU's next seven games – and from the second period against Carolina to the third against Alabama – over a stretch of 32 quarters.

Whether it was all the fault of Jefferson or that of a mad scientist-type offensive coordinator who tossed a complex playbook at a kid who spent his first two years as the youngest starting quarterback in the Southeastern Conference is hard to say. But ever since Jefferson was thrown into the fire as a true freshman in 2008 just past his 18th birthday, inconsistency at the position had been an LSU hallmark.

Consider: In the seven 2010 regular-season games after the opener against the Tar Heels, Jefferson passed (50-of-102, a 48.8 percent completion ratio) for a total of 472 yards, no touchdowns and seven interceptions, and didn't once exceed a hundred yards. In LSU's six other games, including UNC, the Cotton Bowl, some of the Tigers' better opponents (Alabama, Ole Miss and Arkansas), Jefferson went 68-107 (63.5 percent) for 965 yards, seven touchdowns and two interceptions.

In Jefferson's up-and-down adventure, particularly early, no one could be sure week-to-week what to expect, a solidly-managed offense or an uneven performance that the Tiger defense and special teams would have to overcome.

* * *

Jefferson was yanked into the limelight by the tentacles of happenstance. Same with Jefferson's backup, Jarrett Lee.

LSU was handcuffed for a couple of seasons in large measure because Coach Les Miles did not recruit more than one quarterback in the incoming class of 2005, his first haul after taking over from Nick Saban, who had left for the NFL's Miami Dolphins. The hotshot high school quarterback, not only of Louisiana but the nation, was Ryan Perrilloux of East St. John near New Orleans. Everyone but Saban, who seemed to think Perrilloux could be a distraction for his team, was drooling for his services.

After originally committing to Texas, after he came aboard Miles put on a full-court press for Perrilloux' signature, and ultimately got it. But Perrilloux was a problem child who was constantly finding trouble. After playing a key backup role in LSU's 2007 national championship team, Perrilloux finally had to be booted from the team before the next season. "This might be my chance to start as a freshman," Jefferson said he thought at the time. "At the time I hadn't heard of anyone else behind Perrilloux," he said.

It took a while, but he got what he wished for. Redshirt freshman Jarrett Lee, a strong-armed Texan who was supposed to spend 2008 standing on the sidelines and learning, was thrust into the starting lineup a year ahead of time, sharing time with Harvard transfer and injury-prone Andrew Hatch. That plan didn't work out, with Lee passing for 13 touchdowns—and 16 interceptions, an amazing 7 being returned for opposing touchdowns.

After a Lee injury, Jefferson was shoved into the same untenable situation as his predecessor.

* * *

Twelve months earlier it seemed as if Jefferson was a recruiting after-thought for LSU. He didn't play half of his junior season at Destrehan High, just 10 miles away from Perrilloux' old school. He broke his wrist on the helmet of on-coming defensive lineman Drake Nevis, later a teammate at LSU. But as a senior the 6-foot-5 Jefferson quarterbacked Destrehan to a 15-0 record and the state championship, completing 64 percent of his passes.

"I went to a camp at LSU and had a very good workout," he recalled. "I know I caught their eye, the coaches told me they really liked me. But nobody offered me a grant-in-aid, or even indicated they might."

Jefferson's possible services did intrigue others. Invited for a visit to Alabama by new coach Nick Saban, the former Tiger mentor, Jefferson was standing on the 'Bama sidelines for the 2007 game with the Bayou Bengals. The LSU coaches spotted him there, lolling with other Crimson Tide prospects. "I definitely think LSU suddenly became more interested when they saw me in Tuscaloosa," he said with a smile.

Less than two weeks later, LSU offered Jefferson a grant-in-aid and he accepted.

That was the start of his up-and-down college career. Offensive coordinator Gary Crowton, once the offensive-minded head coach at Louisiana Tech, Brigham Young and even the Chicago Bears, loved dabbling with intricate mix-and-match formations and plays. But Crowton was more of a game-strategist than a developer of quarterbacks. Crowton did a brilliant job in the 2007 national title season, but he also had a fifth-year senior in Matt Flynn who was already prepared to direct the LSU offense.

Jefferson, 3 months after reaching his right to vote, was essentially still learning the way to Tiger Stadium and needed help in his growth behind center. "I was just trying to learn the plays and how to read defenses," he said. "You come in and think you're ready to play, but it hits you at once."

* * *

Starting at least a year ahead of schedule, the athletic Jefferson took the reins for Lee. In doing so, he became LSU's youngest starting quarterback in 63 years. Not since a kid named Y.A. Tittle opened the 1945 season had so much responsibility been placed on the shoulder pads of such a youthful Tiger.

His insertion brought fair results. LSU lost 31-30 at Arkansas, giving the Tigers a disheartening 7-5 regular season record. Then, in an outstanding effort by Jefferson in the Peach Bowl, beat Georgia Tech 38-3. Jefferson was the bowl's Offensive MVP, and cumulatively for the experiment of 2008 was 36-of-73 with four touchdowns and one interception.

Things were looking good. Until 2009.

Jefferson was essentially the same project he had been as a freshman. As the full-time starter, the Tigers finished 9-4 but lost to every one of its better opponents, Florida (13-3), Alabama (24-15), Ole Miss (25-23) and Penn State (19-17). An inability to make quick decisions, to look off primary receivers, and a lack of pocket presence leading to a tendency to holding the ball too long were blamed. A good runner, sometimes Jefferson seemed too anxious to bail out of the pocket. Out of the 120 Division I programs, LSU was glaringly ranked 112th in passing offense. Jefferson was 182-296 for 2,166 yards, 17 touchdowns and seven interceptions. His quarterback efficiency rating was 137.18 – 36th in the country.

Today Jordan will acknowledge he perhaps didn't work as hard as he could have. When Miles started utilizing Lee more, playing the backup in seven games and starting one, Jefferson also realized his position was in jeopardy.

* * *

Jefferson played well at times in 2010, not so well at other times. In the quarterback efficiency ratings he actually regressed, slipping to a 114.65.

His backup, Lee, directly accounted for two of LSU's victories. After an early 83-yard touchdown run by Jefferson, Lee was under center most of the day as LSU rolled up 434 yards against Tennessee—a 16-14 game actually won with no time left on the clock when the Vols put in 13 men on defense with LSU at the 1—and then he threw the winning touchdown pass the next week against Florida (33-29) with six seconds remaining.

Then Jefferson ignited in the latter portion of the season, when LSU earned a berth in the 75th Cotton Bowl.

The 9-3 Aggies tied for the top spot of the Big 12 South after beating Oklahoma (33-19) and Nebraska (9-6), and featured a stout defense headlined by linebacker Von Miller, the Butkus Award recipient.

In the first Cotton Bowl ever played in prime time, however, it was Jefferson who hogged the spotlight.

After spotting the Aggies a 10-0 lead, the opening kickoff being returned 69 yards, which led to a short A&M touchdown run, it looked like it might be a long night when Jefferson threw an interception into double coverage at the A&M 2, eventually turning into a 39-yard Aggie field goal.

From that point on, though, Jefferson turned in a tremendous performance, personally accounting for four of LSU's 5 touchdowns and guiding the Tigers to 2 more field goals. He threw 3 scoring passes—all to senior receiver Terrence Toliver for 42, 2 and 41 yards.

He also completed 2 third-down passes keeping touchdown drives alive, and spectacularly, on third-and-19 on LSU's first possession of the second half, Jefferson bolted for 32 yards for a first. That run set up his third touchdown pass.

Jefferson's statistics were not overwhelming—10 completions in 19 attempts for 158 yards, including the touchdown throws—but he was in complete control. LSU converted on nine of 15 third down situations and steered the Tigers to scores on seven of their 12 possessions. LSU had to punt just once.

Reflecting back on the Cotton Bowl, Jefferson said, "I think that was the best game I ever played."

Jefferson came under the tutelage of Steve Kragthorpe as he entered his senior season, where a combination of maturity and a honing of his skills were expected to lift the quarterback to further, and more consistent, heights.

But his coach, Les Miles, said there's more to the total package than just physical improvement. "I just think," Miles said simply, "Jordan Jefferson is a winner."